HAÏTI–

HAÏTI–HAITII?

Philosophical Reflections for Mental Decolonization

BY

JEAN-BERTRAND ARISTIDE

TRANSLATED BY MILDRED ARISTIDE

To Betty Abena Appleby,
In solidarity. From
Haiti, to Detroit and
Africa

M. Aristide
3. 31. 2017

PARADIGM PUBLISHERS
Boulder & London

Copyright © 2011 by Paradigm Publishers

Published in the United States by Paradigm Publishers, 2845 Wilderness Place, Boulder, CO 80301 USA.

Paradigm Publishers is the trade name of Birkenkamp & Company, LLC, Dean Birkenkamp, President and Publisher.

Library of Congress Cataloging-in-Publication Data

Aristide, Jean-Bertrand.
Haiti-Haitii? : philosophical reflections for mental decolonization / Jean-Bertrand Aristide ; translated by Mildred Aristide.
p. cm.
In Kreyol, with English translations.
A collection of poetry, prose, proverbs, and aphorisms.
ISBN 978-1-61205-053-9 (hardback : alk. paper)—ISBN 978-1-61205-054-6 (pbk. : alk. paper)
1. Haiti—Poetry. 2. Haiti—Literary collections. I. Aristide, Mildred, 1962– II. Title.
PM7854.H39A75 2011
841'.914—dc23

2011021279

Printed and bound in the United States of America on acid-free paper that meets the standards of the American National Standard for Permanence of Paper for Printed Library Materials.

Designed & Typeset by Straight Creek Bookmakers in Adobe Caslon.

15 14 13 12 11   1 2 3 4 5

~ *Contents* ~

CONTENTS

Molefi Kete Asante

Foreword

In one report it is said that Toussaint Louverture had wished that his competitor Dessalines would join the revolution and support the struggle for liberation. As Toussaint engaged in battle after battle against the enemies of Haiti, defeating the Spanish and the British, he was called to a negotiation by the French, but with guile they trapped, arrested, and transported him to exile. However, when he received word that Dessalines had committed himself to the battle for Haiti's freedom, it is said, that Louverture, erstwhile leader of Haiti, declared, "At last!" Now that President Jean-Bertrand Aristide, the first democratically elected president of Haiti, has written this beautiful poetic treatise of dignity and nobility in honor of his people, our people, humanity, we can say what millions of Haitians have been waiting to say, "At last!"

Jean-Bertrand Aristide, a charismatic Catholic priest, was first elected to the presidency of Haiti on December 16, 1990, lifting the veil from the political arena in Haiti where the Duvalierists were preparing to return to power. Aristide was the first democratically elected president in the country's history. This landmark victory, with Aristide winning 65% of the vote, was celebrated by the masses of Haitians as a clarion call for reform. Aristide went to work immediately to alleviate the suffering of the poor, to eradicate corruption, to return Haiti to the family of nations as a mature, dignified, and capable nation. Angered by the outpouring of popular support for Aristide, the powerful economic sector sought to slow the social transformation in the country. Aristide had demonstrated that the grassroots issues of the poor, and of his church community, the Ti Legliz, were at the core of Haiti's political life. They also knew that Aristide had been an outspoken critic of the previous government and that his stature had grown when an armed group, with the military watching, attacked his church, St. Jean Bosco, in September 1988. Thirteen members of the church were killed and 70 were hurt in the attack as armed gangs stormed the church and burned it to the ground. They knew, therefore, that the priest who defied the traditional giants of the society had no fear. He set about his work of ridding the country of ethnic, racial, and color prejudice; vowing to level the economic playing field for the masses; reducing military abuses against the population; interrupting drug trafficking; and fighting all forms of human rights abuses. Indeed, he also balanced the federal budget for the first time that anyone could remember. In his words, his goal was to move the country from misery to poverty with dignity.

In spite of these achievement and perhaps because of them, seven months into his first term, in September 1991, a coup d'état led by Duvalierist elements in the military tossed the nation into turbulence with more than 5,000 people killed and the president eventually sent into exile. The traditional ruling elite, the lions of Pétionville, the remnants of Tonton Macoutes, and the upper classes, did not stand for reform that included empowering the masses. Aristide was in exile from 1991 to 1994; however, during the time of his absence and while the country was run by military leaders, thousands of Haitians sought refuge in the United States, risking their lives to cross the ocean in a variety of vessels, most hardly seaworthy, to reach Florida.

In 1994, after considerable political diplomacy, sanctions, and boycotts, the United Nations and the U.S. Army returned President Aristide to Haiti. The unconstitutional Haitian coup leaders were allowed to leave the country as President Bill Clinton dispatched troops in Haiti. The United Nations forces remained in the country supposedly to ensure that the president would have peace in the nation. President Aristide returned to the country and on October 15, 1994, addressed thousands of jubilant Haitians in a moving speech of his vision for the future. During his final 16 months in office President Aristide disbanded the corrupt army of 7,000 soldiers which absorbed 49% of the national budget, and established the first civilian police force. For the first time in their history, Haitians witnessed a peaceful transition from one democratically elected president to the next. After leaving office, he founded the Aristide Foundation for Democracy, dedicated to deepening the roots of Haiti's democracy by opening avenues of participation for all Haitians. Seven years after its founding, the Foundation opened the doors of a medical school. In 2000, President Aristide was again overwhelmingly elected by the Haitian people with 80% of the vote.

In 2004, the Haitian people celebrated their bicentennial of freedom. President Aristide led millions of Haitians in recognition of the country's freedom. Yet as the celebration was happening, on the country's border with the Dominican Republic, armed thugs and former Haitian soldiers stepped up a campaign of terror that included killing government officials and destroying government facilities. On February 29, 2004 President Jean-Bertrand Aristide was essentially kidnapped, taken from his home and placed on a United States plane, accompanied by American military and security agents. Confusion reigned for hours as Haitians and the world community sought to clarify if Aristide had voluntarily given up the presidency or if he had been forced to leave the county by the American government. In the end, political experts in the United States and in Haiti and South Africa saw the removal of the president as forced exile. The President and his wife were flown to Bangui, Central African Republic. After two weeks they went to Jamaica where they were joined by their daughters, and then on to South Africa. An interim de facto government was installed in Haiti under the leadership of Gérard Latorture (a Florida resident brought in from the U.S.) and Boniface Alexandre. As Mildred Aristide is reported to have told Congresswoman Maxine Waters of California and Congressman Charles Rangel of New York, "the coup d'état has been completed." Within a week the Foundation's medical school was seized by the multinational troops in Haiti. The 247 students were removed from the campus and the buildings were transformed into military barracks. Another reign of terror and violence gripped Haiti.

President Aristide's arrival in South Africa in May 2004 offered him an opportunity to increase his knowledge of languages, while exploring the field of neuro-linguistics, as an honorary researcher at the University of South Africa. In addition to Zulu and Swahili, Aristide utilized eight other languages to examine the interactions among multilingualism, memory, and emotion. His previous works in psychology, and more recently in neuro-anatomy at the University of the Witwatersrand, paved the way for such scientific exploration.

At last the organic leader of the Haitian people, Jean-Bertrand Aristide, forcefully and forcibly exiled in South Africa, has spoken the kind word, the sincere concern, the eloquent appeal to sacrifice and sanctity that the people have wanted to hear. The former president of Haiti has written the fascinating and informative book, *Haïti—Haitii?* Who better to write such a revealing book about the culture and people of Haiti than one of the most fascinating and interesting individuals in modern history?

Since President Aristide was kidnapped in 2004, at the beginning of the third century of Haiti's independence, he has been hard at work on several projects. Never one to let time past without effectively capturing its spirit, President Aristide has acquired a Doctorate of Literature and Philosophy in African Languages, mastered several African languages, and taught students in South Africa about overcoming the travails and vicissitudes of life. A man of the people since before his days as the prophet of La Saline, President Aristide has awakened each day with Haiti on his mind and each day he has sought to perfect and prepare himself for service.

This book, *Haïti—Haitii?* is a portrait of two souls, the soul of a man and the soul of a nation. Aristide is a man in service; this has always been his calling, and this book, more than anything else, demonstrates how he has applied this temperament during his time in exile. While he has not engaged in politics, he has been a prime promoter of human rights, systemic decency, and social solidarity with the neglected and unprotected. In essence, he has walked the path of deep devotion to his fellow humans, opening up where he could the closed doors of darkness in order to bring the light of service. We see this in his penetrating style, elegantly constructed verses, and poignant prose. But this book is not merely an aesthetic achievement, which it is; it is profoundly descriptive of the pain, suffering, and victorious consciousness that Aristide embodies. Of course, that is the point; the man and Haiti, Haiti and Aristide are joined in an historic embrace for eternity.

The nation's soul, often exposed, violated, and ridiculed, is also a subject of this book. Haiti is the African's epic against colonialism. It is the pattern, the model, the possibility of victory over oppression; it shows us that the oppressed do not have to remain oppressed forever, and after nearly three hundred years from the 16th century to the 19th century, a people who had been reduced to chattel rose up with an intense dislike for their circumstances and overcame the most modern armies of the era. This is why the author is confident in his celebration of the language that gives us the word "Haitii," and the word "Haiti." Here America comes face-to-face with Africa. This is the meaning, the more profound meaning of the title of this book. I am not sure that the author could have written this book without being touched by the lives of Africans and breathing the air of the continent in every respect. His poetry speaks of his love for Mother Africa.

At the battle of Vertières the determined African men and women rushing to the front of the struggle to end their suffering knew that they did it for posterity. Those who sacrificed their lives, and there were many, were equally the victors with those who claimed independence. This is the meaning of any epic; and to me, *Haïti—Haitii?* has all the elements of an epic. When Heru defeated Set at Edfu and good overcame evil in the ancient narrative of Kemet it was the prologue to Haiti's victory over enslavement and brutality.

Haiti, the pearl of African history, has been rocked by several tragic events during our lifetime. The events that have changed Haiti and challenged (in French, *interpellé*), the United States, Africa, and Europe are the overthrow of President Aristide by tyranny and guile, the earthquake of January 2010, and the cholera outbreak said to have originated with the many foreign troops in the country. Of course, Haiti has received its share of hurricanes, droughts, floods, and petty criminal activity, but the big three events are the ones that must be seen as shattering all expectations in a modern government. To me, the deposing of a president who was popularly elected with an overwhelming majority by external forces because of his progressive policies and calls for justice for his people is the most egregious of the events. The earthquake is something none of us could have prevented; it was a natural disaster of the greatest magnitude. However, cholera did not have to be introduced to the nation. Haiti had been free of cholera for nearly one hundred years and the evidence now suggests that Nepali troops of the United Nations forces inadvertently caused the epidemic. The strand of cholera now in Haiti has been identified as Asian. Nevertheless, I suggest that President Aristide, the beloved leader of the nation, was prepared to serve the nation during the earthquake reconstruction and the cholera outbreak. Who could have rallied the people? Who could have organized the agencies and the NGOs? Who could have stopped the mass looting of the resources of the nation? There is only one voice that the people of Haiti, in general, believe can electrify the masses to do for them what others cannot do for them. The author has shown in this incredibly dynamic book that his writing is as passionate as his speaking. Considered by modern speech scholars as one of the best orators of his generation, the author has brought his love of words, grammar, etymology, and structure to his literary work.

Aristide's book was written in his native Kreyòl, with sections translated by him into Kiswahili, and then translated into English by Mildred Aristide, his brilliant wife, who is an accomplished legal scholar herself. Pointedly, the book is not translated into French. When the author writes,

From 1804 until today / Who continues to suck dry the sap of the country?

he is asking a question that embarrasses those who fail to realize that France owes Haiti more than 21 billion dollars. This is not a rhetorical question, but one that establishes the severity of the burden that the Haitian people have had to bear. There could be no more sensitive literary approach to the horrendous set of circumstances that were devised by human beings than in Aristide's questioning style,

Who orchestrated the military coup d'état in 1991,
Plus the presidential coup d'état kidnapping in 2004,
In order to bury the neo-liberal death plan deeper
In the entrails of Haiti?

The answer to this poetic question and others leads the reader to the conclusion that Haiti's plight is that it has rarely been free of the sticky interventionist fingers of those who have maintained a consistent animus toward the first free black republic in the world. Numerous politicians have ruled Haiti for the interest of their own families or for outside interests. When President Aristide created and led the Fanmi Lavalas to power he had achieved something that was considered impossible; he had resurrected the spirit of the lowest classes and made them the masters of their destiny.

Haiti has never seen a truer democrat than Jean-Bertrand Aristide. No leader since the days when Mackendal and Boukman sought to organize masses has been so committed to the freedom of the people as Aristide. Indeed, the trouble with the ruling classes, as President Barack Obama has seen in the United States, is that they refuse to give up privilege for the benefit of the masses. Unfortunately this situation always sets up the inevitable conflict between justice and injustice, between right and wrong, between liberty and oppression. Aristide cast his lot with the majority of the people and they rewarded him by electing him twice to the highest office in the land. Yet in neither case were the minority rich class and its foreign supporters willing to allow him to complete his term in office. The president-poet has written:

Condemning the small ant for hiding
Inside a coconut while it takes a needed break
Is popular in the courts here.

And we are left thinking that this could be anywhere because wherever there is evil, injustice, and oppression one sees the small, the poor, the unprivileged, and the masses running to hide in the coconut. Aristide names this section "the scissors of legitimate defense" and we are able to read clearly the author's sense of resistance to utter destruction. *Haïti—Haitii?* is a telling documentary written in poetry, proverbs, aphorisms, and prose, an African sort of writing style, indirection, everything is everything, in order to come at the issue from the four cardinal points of the universe.

Finally, in a land of hundreds of artists, none has drawn such a magnificent picture of Haiti's African roots as Aristide. In a land known for its poets, seers, mystics, and religious leaders, no truth has ever been more powerfully impressed on pages than the words of Aristide in *Haïti—Haitii?* If this is not Haiti's epic, or Africa's, then it is surely the epic of a struggle against all odds confronted by the Haitian people. What Dr. Aristide has given us is the exacting word of a reflective, passionate human who sees that good inevitably overcomes evil.

—Molefi Kete Asante,
author of *The History of Africa*

⁓ PART ONE ⁓

A) Introduction

All earthquakes are earthquakes
But there is one that is unparalleled in bringing destruction.
January 12, 2010, in about 35 seconds,
An earthquake unlike any other earthquake turned
Haiti upside down in death, calamity,
Catastrophe, despair, screams and cadavers.

Suddenly several million victims
Were left homeless, without water, without food, without help.
One hundred thousand houses were destroyed, 200,000 others
    damaged.
The National Palace and the Cathedral of Port-au-Prince,
Like the majority of government buildings and churches, were
    devastated.

In the space of 35 seconds 1,350 schools were demolished,
Fifty hospitals destroyed, 90% of Leogane wiped out,
Forty-five percent of Jacmel plus 40% of Port-au-Prince flattened.
In the space of 35 seconds the country lost
More than 10 million American dollars, representing
More than 120% of the gross national product.

Sunday April 4, 2010, a powerful earthquake
Measuring 7.2 hit Mexico.
Results: 2 people died, 100 or so were injured.
And yet the earthquake that hit Haiti
Measured 7.0 and caused nearly 300,000 deaths.

Everywhere, oh, scores of people buried alive,
Smothered to death, torn to pieces, or crushed under cement.
As for the thousands of people gravely wounded,
Heartbreak, anguish, trauma, tears.
Doctors amputated legs or arms without anaesthesia.

This earthquake made television cameras
Across the world focus on Haiti.
Blacks like Whites, young and old
Everywhere suffered with the victims and, there and then,
Many hands joined in solidarity with Haiti.

A beautiful rose of thanks to every person
Who stood up to give birth to this solidarity.
In the face of such a tragedy, Whites who are good Whites
Suffered just like Blacks who are good Blacks.

Unfortunately behind this unprecedented catastrophe
There is a masked game of colonization.
While Whites and Blacks with sensitive hearts want to help Haiti,
The new colonists want to continue to use the country
To, before all else, defend their own interests.

For 400 years, who imposed slavery
In order to suck the country's riches down to its bones? The colonists.
Slavery is a crime against humanity,
But have the victims found reparation? No.

From 1804 until today
Who continues to suck dry the sap of the country? The new colonists.
France owes Haiti more than 21 billion dollars,
But have the victims yet been paid this money? No.

Who orchestrated the military coup d'état in 1991,
Plus the presidential coup d'état kidnapping in 2004,
In order to bury the neo-liberal death plan deeper
In the entrails of Haiti? The new colonists.

This unprecedented catastrophe is neither super-natural,
Nor all-natural, because it is partly the result
Of a colonization that never completely ended.
Moreover, small minded people are about to fall into the trap of
New colonists who have pounced on this tragedy to
Hastily present themselves as the saviors of Haiti.

Long ago colonists trumpeted
That they were bringing **civilization** to the slaves.

Today, the new colonists choose to hide behind
A flag called the Reconstruction of Haiti.

The reconstruction of Haiti! Yes, it is an obligation.
An obligation of the children of the country and of foreigners indebted
  to Haiti.
This reconstruction forces us to look at where we came from
In order to prepare the foundation of a beautiful new Haiti.

The harder the winds of mental decolonization blow,
Smaller are the chances that this reconstruction will drown in a pool of
  shame.
Under the flag of dignity there should be no confusion between
Manifestations of solidarity and the beggars' bowl.

The beggars' bowl hung around the country's neck
Is part of the wider masked plot for colonization.
Unfortunately the country has a *restavèk* president
Wandering about, asking for charity with no dignity —
Against the will of the majority of the children of Haiti.

For more than 200 years the super powers
Have been saying that they have given Haiti millions in charity.
The millions loaned to Haiti at exorbitant interest rates
Are passed off as international aid or charity.

When much of this money was used to buy powerful weapons
For an army of 7,000 soldiers that consumed
Forty percent of the national budget, it seemed normal in
A country with 1.5 doctors for every 11,000 residents.

In reality a few examples are enough to demonstrate clearly
That this money is not there to serve the interest of the majority:

1. Almost half of the money that Haiti owes to foreign banks
   Is money that was borrowed before the 1990 election.

2. In 1991, the World Bank agreed
   To lend Haiti 37 million dollars but
   It was only 6 days before the 1991 coup d'état that

The Bank released 30 of this 37 million.

Thinking people ought to ask why
Was it only 6 days before the coup d'état
That the World Bank decided to release that money?
Because at the time, the Lavalas government
Was going to spend that money in the interest of the people
The Bank held on to it in order to give to the putschists for them
To crush the people and squander with their allies.

Likewise we well understand why
The World Bank loaned
Jean-Claude Duvalier's government, listen carefully,
Two hundred and fifty-six million dollars plus another 158
    million
That went to the military government that
The new colonists put in place after 1986.

3. After the December 16, 1990 election,
    The Inter-American Development Bank agreed to lend the
        country of Haiti
    Only 12 million American dollars.
    But it's the same Inter-American Development Bank that loaned
    The military government 110 million dollars
    Before the December 16 election;
    Plus another 55 million American dollars
    In the year 1990 alone.

    The reason is very clear: they prefer to deal with
    Restavèk governments that suck the life out of the country.
    So, rosy speeches are for the people
    And the bulk of the money is for thieves and plunderers.

4. In November 2003, the IDB agreed
    To lend Haiti 200 million dollars but
    In reality the bulk of that money arrived only
    After the February 29, 2004 kidnapping.

    The reason is very clear: When it's people who are serious
    Who will spend money for the country
    These foreign banks hold on to the money.

When it's thieves who will misuse the money
With their acolytes, no problem.

In good Kreyòl, the pot is lifted on to the stove in the name of
the people,
But it comes down on the backs of big corruption.
Yet this Hebrew proverb is no secret:

אל ההו לההול לשמוד צל השמנה

It means: You don't put a cat in charge of guarding butter.

The country's authorities waste their time begging for charity,
While the country is filled with natural riches like iridium,
Gold, copper, uranium, bauxite, silver, pozzolana, marble …
The calcium carbonate in Payan alone is worth more than 23 million dollars.
The petroleum reserve is perhaps greater than what we believe,
Not counting ourselves, which constitute the country's greatest riches.

Colonists and new colonists consider poor people
Like sweet mangos that they can suck, eat and throw away.
This is why the foreign soldiers who showed up in 2004
And in 2010 did not come to give the poor security.
Colonization is wrapped inside rosy speeches, beautiful promises
While weapons are there to defend the interests of the new colonists.

About 10 months after the unprecedented earthquake,
1,600,000 victims are still languishing in the streets, without homes,
Without protection, without help, without hope.
There, on the ground, in mud, the rain wets them, the sun dries them,
Rats climb on top of them, flies and roaches cover them
Because they are parked underneath pieces of tarp, fabric, or a tent.

The sting of mosquitoes has replaced
The sting of malaria and tetanus vaccinations.
Clumps of mud have replaced ointments for rashes and sores.
Dirty rags have replaced bandages at the ends of foot and leg stubs,
Hand and arm stubs, where doctors cut without anaesthesia.

Demagogic political promises substitute psychological counselling.
While the cholera epidemic has already killed more than 1000 people,

Not counting close to 15,000 people contaminated by the disease.
This is the first time in a century for cholera to hit the country.

This upside down picture is a mirror image of a Haiti suspended
    upside down.
This upside down picture shows clearly how the new colonists
Keep Haiti upside down, while they talk of reconstruction.
Be it the meaning of Haiti, be it the philosophy hidden behind it,
The new colonists don't want to know it and don't try to know it.

This upside down landscape does not indicate
The road to Haiti's reconstruction.
This upside down landscape points in the direction of recolonization
Under the trumpet call for billions of dollars in charity
In order to rebuild other walls of apartheid after 206 years of
    independence.

After 206 years of independence

After 206 years of independence
Haiti continues to sacrifice
Morning, noon and night to pour
The fuel of liberty in its lamp of dignity.

After 206 years of liberty
Haiti still pays because
It dared risk death
In purging both slavery and colonists
To give liberty to all people.

Even today the new colonists
Have yet to accept this victory.
Years have come and gone,
Centuries have changed,
But the new colonists have not changed.

For them Haiti should not have a
True political independence
That is wound tightly to
A genuine economic independence.

This way they can always use lackeys,
Sycophants or mental slaves at home

To stop the Haitian People from living
With liberty, equality and fraternity.

The last coup d'état kidnapping
They masterminded on 29 February 2004,
Proved clearly how they refuse
To respect the will of the Haitian People.

A will that springs and gushes from
The essence of the root of the word Haiti itself.
The conventional definition of Haiti
As *the land of mountains*
Blocks the elites and most intellectuals
From going further.

On the 207th anniversary
Of Haiti's independence
There is a critically important question
Which merits a critically important answer:
What does the word Haiti mean?

People who are experts in history
Know that Haiti is the mother of liberty
Because it is the first place where slaves
Achieved a never before seen revolution in 1804
To break the chains of slavery.

In the entire world, it is the only slave revolution
That succeeded in giving birth to liberty.
People who are experts in history know this
And naturally, people who are civilized understand
The importance of liberty in the lives of all peoples.

Civilized people do not judge others based on the color of their skins.
Civilized people cannot think like racists.
Civilized people respect the liberty of all people.
Where civilized Blacks and Whites stand together
To eradicate, uproot, deracinate racist weeds,
Ah! Yes, the roots of liberty grow like mushrooms.

It is the marrow of this civilization that we discover
In the good relations that Toussaint Louverture had

With Whites who understood that liberty was meant for everyone.
Thankfully today there still are civilized Whites and Blacks
Who stand together for the rise of liberty across the entire country.

If Haiti is the mother of liberty it is normal
For us to scrutinize both its birth certificate and its history
Until we find the answer to this question:
What does the word Haiti mean for us?

To answer this profound question
We chose a style of language
That combines 2 strengths: poetry and philosophy.
One complements the other in achieving the task.

This poetry draws its inspiration
From a poem in the languages Swahili and Kreyòl
That we titled: Haïti—Haitii.
Further, we utilized a hundred or so proverbs
From Swahili itself.

The analysis of proverbs
Is a science called paremiology.
We examine it under a philosophic microscope that
Fastens the umbilical cord of the word Haiti to
The core of the entrails of Mother Africa.
If we speak of Mother Africa, we are speaking exactly of
The mother of a philosophy called *Ubuntu*.

Philosophy of *Ubuntu*

The philosophy of *Ubuntu*[1] is embodied in three key words:
Umuntu ngumuntu ngabantu, which mean:
A person is a person through other human beings.
A person becomes a person through the community.
A person is person when she/he treats others well.

In the philosophy of *Ubuntu* there is no room for
Selfishness or egocentricity.
A person's existence is intertwined with the community.

---

1. Ubuntu is a Zulu word that means "humanity."

So that the philosophy of *Ubuntu* is the source of all philosophy
Grounded in solidarity, cooperation, unity
Respect, dignity, justice, liberty and love of the other.

From Epikouros,
Founder of one of the largest schools of philosophy
In Greece 300 years before the birth of Christ,
To philosophers Socrates, Aristotle, Plato and others,
All these thinkers came long after *Ubuntu.*
The philosophic thread that dominated the theology of the first
    Christians
Was a love that resembled very much the philosophy of *Ubuntu.*

There, in *Ubuntu,* Africans found
An unmatched strength to resist slavery.
The children of Africa were certain that all people were possessed of dignity
And so no one should treat anyone like an animal.

Days go, days come. Development of the scientific foundation
Of the philosophy of *Ubuntu* has shed a ray of light for
People looking to understand the meaning of the word Haiti.
The philosophy of *Ubuntu* transcends the anatomical difference
That exists between a human brain and an animal brain.

The importance of this vision forces us to pause
In order to decipher the logic of this reasoning:
It has been now almost 2 million years since the human brain
Evolved to the level of Homo habilis.

Homo habilis means able man.
Instead of walking on four feet,
The evolution of the brain allowed Homo habilis
To walk on two feet.

This allowed the front feet to serve
As hands to make tools, to eat…
Homo habilis's brain was not at all heavy.
It weighed about 500 grams.

Later, when Homo habilis got stronger, more skilled
In walking on two feet, they named him

In Latin, Homo erectus, meaning
Person walking erect on two feet.
Homo erectus's brain weighed 808 grams.

When his brain grew to weigh 1400 grams,
They changed his name to call him Homo sapiens.
Homo sapiens means person who is wise, intelligent.
They were the ones who came from Africa, went to Asia
To cross over to America, and arrive in Haiti by foot.

They were able to travel by foot because at the time
There was no Bering Strait separating
The Asian continent from the American continent.
It has been approximately 30 to 15 million years
Since they made this great voyage.

Our brain is also the brain of the Homo sapiens.
It is twice as heavy as the brain of chimpanzees and gorillas.
Even if the elephant's brain is heavier than the human brain,
It is because of the elephant's body size, it is nothing compared
To the wondrous power of the human brain.

In the 10 years preceding 1 January 1804,
A series of intellectuals, like Galvani, Aldini and Volta,
Alexander von Humboldt … debated extensively
The amount of electrical energy in any brain,
Be it a human brain or an animal brain.

This brings us exactly to the anatomical difference
That the philosophy of *Ubuntu* embraces, only to transcend it.

Why is there an enormous difference
Between a human brain and the brain of an animal?

Both for a person and for an animal,
The back of the brain is called the cerebellum
And the front of the brain is called the cerebrum.
But in the animal's brain, the cerebrum
Does not develop as it does in the human brain.

The cerebrum is the epicenter of
Reasoning, thought, calculation, knowledge, intelligence …
Thankfully, in the human brain, walking on two feet
Played a big role in the development of the cerebrum.

If this enormous difference is necessary and important
In distinguishing a person from an animal,
It is not sufficient for the philosophy of *Ubuntu* wherein
"Umuntu ngumuntu ngabantu."
A person is a human being through other people.
People become persons through the community.
A person is a human being when he or she treats others well.

The power of poetry

"Umuntu ngumuntu ngabantu."
These three African words ring like
Three musical notes that resonate in a perfect chord to interpret
A musical partition called:
Philosophic poetry: Haïti—Haitii.

Poetry squeezes eloquence from words,
Poetry has the energy to alter brain waves.
So it's not surprising that a Latin poet
Named Publius Ovidius once declared that
The beautiful poems of Titus Lucretius would die,
Only if the entire world were to disappear.

When a poet captures the vibration of emotion,
He discovers the sensitive signal where
Emotions are recorded in the human brain;
Sensitive signals that come from areas of the brain
Such as the hippocampus, the amygdale, the VPC, the DPC.[2]

When these signals are in balance with human reason,
The words of proverbs bloom a philosophy of love,
Words of liberation move to a higher level,
Words of decolonization make our dignity blossom,

---

2. VPC is the abbreviation for Ventromedial prefrontal cortex; DPC stands for Dorsolateral prefrontal cortex

Beautiful words and truth walk hand in hand
So that the eyes and ears can discover the light of *Ubuntu*.

The rendezvous is announced, today, in this light,
For us to answer this big question:
What does the word Haiti mean for us?

I wish with all my heart
That this philosophical poetry offers
A small contribution to help
The wings of dignity sprout feathers of liberty
Under a giant flag called
MENTAL DECOLONIZATION.

Poem

Haïti—Haitii

Watu wengi wanajua jina la nchi yetu ni Haïti.
Lakini watu wachache wanaelewa maana yake.
Ndiyo, Haïti, maana yake ni nini? Ni nini?

Many people know that the name of our country is Haïti.
But not many understand what this name means.
Yes, Haïti, what does it mean?
Where do the roots of this word come from?

Kwa upande wa mababu na wazee,
Haïti, kwa dhati, ni jina njema sana.
Hata sasa, jina hili hung'ara gizani
Kwa kweli, Haïti, maana yake ni nini?

For our great, great grandparents, or ancestors,
Haïti is veritably a beautiful name.
Still today the name glows in the darkness
Truly, what does the word Haïti mean?

Laiti watu wengi waligundua mizizi yake,
Ingekuwa rahisi kutambua maana yake.
Tukitamka Haïti, tutakumbuka Afrika.

If only people were to uncover its roots,
It would be easy to understand the meaning of the word.
Once we pronounce Haïti we remember Africa.

Kutoka wakati ule wazungu walianza
Kuwatumia waAfrika kama watumwa,
Mama Afrika aliadimisha, kwa kweli,
Nguvu, bidii na fahari za watoto wake.

Since the time that white colonists began
To use Africans to turn Africans into slaves,
With all her heart, Mama Africa has been celebrating
The courage, strength and pride
Of the children of her entrails.

Kwa nguvu zote, waAfrika walisema:
Hapana! Hapana! **Hai ! Hai ! Hai !**
Hatutaki kuondoka kwenye ardhi yetu.
Tunakataa kata kata. Tunakataa kata kata.

With great courage, Africans declared:
No! No! **Do not! Do not! Do not! Do not! Do not**!
We do not want, we do not want to leave our land.
We refuse completely, we refuse forever.

Kwa nguvu sana, waAfrika walisema:
Ati! Sio kweli? Tunaona nini? Ni nini?
Hatutaki. Hatutaki kupoteza uhuru yetu.
Tunakataa kata kata. Tunakataa kata kata.

With great courage, Africans declared:
What! This is not true! What is this?
We do not, we do not want to lose our liberty.
We refuse completely, we refuse forever.

Tangu siku zile mpaka kufika Haïti,
Wa Afrika waliendelea ku sisitiza:
Ni lazima tupate uhuru kwasababu
Ni bora kufa kuliko kuwa mtumwa.

Since then, and until they reached Haïti,
Africans continued to affirm and to repeat:
We must seize our liberty, because
We rather death over slavery.

Wazungu wote watatutesa!
Hai*dhuru!*
Wazungu watatuhuzunisha!
Hai*tuudhi!*
Wazungu watakuwa
Na watumwa siku zote?
Hai*wezekani.*
Wazungu wote watatuua!
Hai*dhuru.*
Kufa ni bora kuliko utumwa.

The white colonists will persecute us!
Not a problem!
The white colonists will torture us!
Not a problem!
The white colonists will always have slaves?
Not possible!
The white colonists will kill us?
Not a problem!
We prefer death to slavery.

Kwa hivyo sisi tunasema:
Hai *!* **Hai** *!* **Hai** *!* **Hai** *!*
*Temeamuwa kuto ku***tii**
Tii, tii, tii, tii, tii, tii *…*
Mpaka sisi sote tupate uhuru.

That is why we say:
Not! Not! Not! Not! Not! Not!
Resolutely, we have decided not to **obey,**
Obey, obey, obey, obey …
Until we all seize our liberty.

Tunaapa, tunaapa,
Kuna maneno mawili:
Ya kwanza, **Hai.**

Ya pili, **Tii.**
Kwa kifupi: **Haitii.**

We swear,
And swear again,
There are 2 words:
First, **Not**
Second, **Obey**
Therefore, **Do not obey**
In Swahili: **Haitii,**
Which means: **Do not obey.**

Kwa hivyo, tuseme:
Haitii. Haitii. Haitii.
Mpaka tupate uhuru.
Ndiyo hapo jina
La nchi yetu litakuwa
HAITI.

This is why we say:
Haïti, Haitii, Haitii,
Until we become free.
Then truly, will
Our country's name be
HAÏTI.

B) Reflections

Victims and butchers

On this path where poetry encounters science in a search for the roots of the word Haïti, there is another question that must be immediately posed: when the slaves cried "Haitii, Haitii," do not obey, do not obey the colonists, didn't that cause the colonists to respond with greater brutality?

When we say slave and colonist, we mean victim and butcher. Or rather, we should specify, victim under the domination of an oppressor. Our responsibility, before all else, is to put ourselves in the position of the victims to try and understand their tribulations, indignation and suffering.

Adhabu ya kaburi aijua maiti. The torment of the grave is known only by the corpse. Only the tip of the knife knows what lies in the heart of the yam.

When, morning, noon and night, the slaves cried: "Haitii, Haitii," the message was clear: their greatest dream was not to lessen the brutality and savagery of the colonialists, but rather to end slavery, seize their freedom so that they could live.

This determination demonstrates how the fires of suffering can sear the womb but fail to burn ideas in the minds of defiant black women and men. While these fires were like the flames of hell against their bodies, their spirits embraced inspirational thoughts leading them to the path of paradise.

Nadhari njia ya peponi. Good judgment is the road to paradise.

Choosing to obey the colonists meant deciding to stay in hell. This is what the slaves believed, from the moment that the colonists' dogs attacked them, devouring their flesh as they were dragged to the white colonists newly arrived in Africa to kidnap Africans morning, noon and night.

Operation kidnapping

Operation kidnapping was a complex enterprise that the whites put in place to capture everyone and anyone they wanted. They landed in the middle of the night with heavy arms, ferocious dogs to set upon innocent people who were asleep in their homes after a hard day's work.

Suddenly, homesteads were encircled; people were awakened with the strike of a cudgel. Kicked down, clubbed to submission, the innocent were roped and chained like beasts.

Sometimes, it was not only a homestead that the whites kidnapped, but an entire village before setting the community alight to show unmistakeably that operation kidnapping was more savage than the most ferocious of beasts.

As for the innocent going about their business during the day, best that they not find themselves where the whites were operating, else they too would fall victim. Waiting was either a rope to harness the captives, or dogs to drag them as prey. Dogs that were wild; trained to either capture or devour humans.

After operation kidnapping it is then that the victims begin to walk, and walk, and walk, and walk and walk, before being shoved into trenches, in the middle of nowhere. Those who speak English call this place a slave pen. Lacking a roofless house or any sort of lean-to, they dumped the slaves under an old tree.

To get here the victims walked one behind the other, arms bound with heavy ropes, feet shackled one to the other. Often, the whites placed a tree limb under their necks that sheared across their skin like a razor blade. Under these conditions, escape was impossible.

The line of slaves snaked several kilometers long. When a slave tired and fell, there were whips to force him to rise. For those who fell but did not rise, there were dogs and wild beasts ready to gorge. Piles of bones littered the route. Creatures came from far to eat fresh meat. This special feast could extend over weeks or months.

The flesh of children was not spared; usually, most were first to die. To drag them along, the whites tied them securely to tattered rags, attempting to pose as their mothers' skirts. When a child made it to the slave pen that was one more slave for the auctioneer's block; if not it still meant one more meal for the wild beasts. Only a slave mother could describe this searing pain.

Isipokuwasha hujairamba. If it doesn't burn you it's because you haven't tasted it.

Operation kidnapping deployed another inhuman tactic: separating mother from child, husbands from their wives, sisters from brothers, cousins from one another, to better victimize them. There were many slave pens to dish out this separation.

If in one area there were more victims or slaves than there were slave pens, the butchers dumped the surplus loads under towering trees where the rain drenched them, the sun parched them, and nightfall covered them like animals. As for the blows of clubs, kicks, lashes and strikes, they were meted out at any time and for any reason. There was no different treatment afforded people who were kidnapped and people who had been purchased here and there to be piled one on top of the other.

Flesh torn by vicious dogs, bleeding wounds, gashes carved from the strike of the chain, provoked haemorrhaging, wounds, and cracked skulls spewing blood — causing a decay and decomposition made to look like rotting corpses.

The innocent spent weeks or months in these depots before being dumped into the holds of the slave ships bound for their journey to their endless exile. An exile that no doubt darkened even a moonless night.

Jambo usilolijua ni kama usiku wa giza. A matter about which you know nothing is like a dark night.

On a ship called the Henrietta Marie, like on all other slave ships, the nights were already pitch-black for the up to 200 slaves that filled every available space. The left foot of every man shackled to the right foot of another.

One on top of the other, stacked high, chained above, chained below, men, women and children in the bowels of a hell-boat not knowing where they would be unloaded, or for how long they would continue to burn in this fire of death. In 1784, by the River Congo, 500 Africans were loaded on board a boat named Larouchelle, destined to disembark in St. Domingue, like animals for market.

Pounding waves, nausea, vomiting, diarrhoea, suffocation, heart attacks, nervous breakdowns, fears, screams, tremors, terror, high blood pressure, low blood pressure: people died like flies: one in every 3 slaves carried in the cauldron of the criminals' boat died. Many managed to fight, break through the chains and, in a rage, hurl themselves into the ocean to be delivered from the colonists.

It is under these conditions that whites kidnapped and transported Africans to the shores of America and the Caribbean. Some experts estimate that at least 20 million Africans were taken; others estimate that it was more than 100 million. Regardless of the real number, this crime was too much when committed against one person, let alone when committed against the millions of innocent people grilled in this oven. One minute was already too much for anyone to bear as a slave on board this floating hell called the Henrietta Marie. Yet this voyage could last 7, 8 or 9 months.

During a long period in the 15th century, some among the wealthy of Portugal controlled these expeditions. But afterward, for several centuries, it was the wealthy authorities of France, England and Spain who controlled this never before seen trade.

Notwithstanding the trauma, pain and unimaginable suffering already endured by slaves after the unleashing of operation kidnapping, the end of the hellish voyage at sea meant a greater hell on another land. The whips and cudgels of the colonists were to become more powerful than ever. For the victims, the message was crystal clear.

Siku njema huonekana asubuhi. A good day is apparent in the morning.

That is why the victims never tire saying "Haitii, Haitii!" Meaning: Do not obey the colonist until we have seized our liberty! This extraordinary resistance was the antithesis of the Black Code that Louis XIV imposed as law to continue to repress the slaves. Although slavery and operation kidnapping began in 1492, the Black Code was enacted in March 1685. A short perusal of the code is enough to understand that to be truly free, the victims had only one option.

C) The Black Code:

A black cord to hang blacks
Because whites invented a black code intended to kill blacks,
All the great spirits of liberty rallied around the only option:
The one option to cut the black cord: they said no.
"No, **Haitii, do not obey** the colonists until we are free."

Reflections

Article 1

" ... *Drive all the Jews from the colonies* ... "

Tribulations and tribulations

The first article in the black code requires the authorities to drive out all Jews living on the diverse islands that the French whites had seized. Was

it in the slaves' interest that the colonists took this decision? No; it had
nothing to do with the slaves' interests, which means:

Kuni ya juu uchaga haicheki iliyo motoni. Firewood at the top of a burning
pile does not laugh at the pieces of wood beneath it.

On 31 March 1492, the Catholic king and queen of Spain Isabella the 1st
of Castile and Ferdinand II of Aragon published the Alhambra Decree
giving Jews two options: Either convert to Catholicism or leave Spain
before the 31 of July 1492. Thousands of Jews ended up in many other
countries, such as Portugal, Brazil, Guadeloupe, Martinique ... In the year
1496, the king of Portugal drove the Jews from Portugal too. By 1685 this
persecution had increased when Louis XIV expelled the Jew pursuant to
the first article of the black code.

At that time, was there any connection between this decision and the
slaves? None really; but it offers a good opportunity to remember this
lesson: when Jews recount their tribulations, powerful elites say "Bravo!
That is history." When the poor recount their tribulations, powerful elites
say "Be quiet! That is vengeance." Guilty colonists who never forget always
want to remind the innocent that: *Sahau ni dawa ya waja.* Forgetting is
the medicine of humanity.

Article 2

*"... All the slaves who will be in our islands will be baptized
and educated in the catholic, apostolic and Roman Church ... "*

The weapon of religion

In the eyes of those who do not see well, religion looks like gold. Thankfully, those with sound and analytical minds know that: *Yote yang'aayo si
dhahabu.* Not everything that sparkles is gold.

Since time immemorial, many of the powerful elites have used religion
as a potent weapon: a weapon to deconstruct, destroy, dismember the
ideas of others while forcing their own ideas onto those with stunted
brains to subjugate and break those persons, and utilize them for their
own purposes.

In this way, religion came to resemble a weapon of war. In addition to other deadly weapons, the white colonists carefully selected the Catholic religion as an evil weapon with which to wage war. *Bila silaha usiingie vitani.* Do not go to war without weapons.

So, automatically baptism lost its true meaning, just like a coconut that has lost its milk and pulp. While the limbs of slaves were shackled in slavery, the colonists turned religion into a sacred chain to try and lock the minds of slaves in a blackout of fear.

Again and again, the slaves heard that there was a horse (evil spirit) in their minds that prevented them from obeying the master. The solution was baptism to drive out this horse and make the slave docile.

After a first baptism, slaves who continued to disobey were forced to be baptized a second time to again try and rid them of the horse. Strange or cynical, there were some innocent victims who the colonists forcefully baptized 7, 8, 9 times.

All disobedient slaves were considered savages needing baptism. Are there indeed many true savages? Yes, there are. Really? Yes, the true savages were these colonists.

Asiyeona aibu zake asione za mwenziwe. One who does not see his own failings should not see those of others.

Of course this truth had no relevance to the colonists: What counted was to use religion to break the slaves.

Article 3

"... We forbid public exercise of religions other than the Catholic, apostolic and Roman one ..."

There is religion and there is religion

From 1562 to 1598 in the country of France, Catholics and Protestants fought 8 wars. Blood was spilled, heads chopped off, many Protestants were assassinated. August 24, 1572, on the day of the feast of St.

Barthélemy, in the city of Paris, in France, Catholics massacred Protestants, turning the waters of the river Seine red.

Because the massacre lasted several days, dead bodies were everywhere. Whether it was killings committed during the Crusade (1095–1291) or killings committed in the horrific massacre of St Barthélemy, they all demonstrate how ferocious the Catholic Church was with its opponents.

Dalili ya mvua ni mawingu. Clouds signal rain.

Article 3 of the black code did not come as a surprise to Protestants. But certainly, it was a major pronouncement that served to displace and uproot Protestantism, like all other religions, except Roman Catholicism. For all peoples in the world spiritual belief is like the root of a tree. To cut the belief that a people have in their tradition and culture is not an undertaking that civilized people can take lightly.

The only riches that the slaves were able to bring with them from Africa were precisely the roots of their beliefs, traditions, religion, culture, history, languages and all the other roots of remembrances buried deep in their memories anchored firmly, like an umbilical cord, to the entrails of Mother Africa, always alive in their spirit.

Kelele za chura hazimkatazi ng'ombe kunywa maji. The noise of a frog does not stop the cow from drinking water.

Article 3 could prevent the slaves from freely professing their religion but it could not stop them from drawing from the source of their belief. Every religion is a religion, but for the slaves, not all were the same. For them, the religion of the colonists was like a fist attempting to grasp water.

Konzi ya maji haifumbatiki. A fist cannot grasp water.

The ability of slaves to understand religion rests in this profound truth: illiterate but not stupid. If the slaves did not completely sever the roots of their African religion, it is because they believed that they could neither cut the roots of their own existence, nor kneel, head bent, eyes closed and mistake the moon for a giant piece of cheese.

For Roman Catholicism to be truly good, it had to stop acting like a mother with two breasts: one sweet, one bitter; the sweet one for the colonists, the bitter one for the slaves. In the eyes of the slaves, the coffee of colonists' religion was unfiltered, leaving behind too many coffee grinds.

Article 4

"... If you are not a Roman apostolic Catholic, you cannot have the rank of chief slave ... "

Religion of cadavers or Catholicism?

The emphasis put on Roman apostolic Catholicism signals the importance of this weapon in colonization. Long ago in the year 146 before the birth of Jesus Christ the Romans used the weapon of religion to try and subjugate Africa. It was the first time that they invaded and succeeded in taking Africa, grabbing the city of Carthage in the country of Tunisia.

In 106 after the birth of Jesus Christ, the flag of religion was raised and floated arrogantly across the imperialistic Roman Empire that measured 5.9 million square kilometres under the Roman emperor Trajan. Then, the imperialist Romans were all powerful. From the north of Africa, to different territories of Europe, they ruled, repressed, controlled, dominated in the name of the gods that they served.

When this mighty power roared, it was like a wild beast, devouring any and all foreign religions in its path. Emperor Constantine committed unthinkable atrocities against the first Christians. But in the year 312, once converted to Christianity he mounted religion, like one mounts a horse, to defend his own interests. The Roman apostolic church indeed became the religion of the state.

If Jesus were to be born a second time and to return on earth he would again proclaim the good news of liberation and the powerful elite of the state and the church would again plot to accuse him, judge him, condemn him and assassinate him a second time.

The interests of the colonists and the interests of Jesus are two mountains that will never meet. Slavery and liberty are exactly like hell and paradise. Because illiterate does not mean stupid, the slaves did not have to pore over the words of a Catechism tailored to serve one set of interests, in order to understand the religion of the colonists.

La kuvunda halina ubani. The stench of rot cannot be camouflaged by incense.

Article 5

*"..Protestantism can never impede the progress of
apostolic Roman Catholicism ... "*

Religion as bait

The Protestant church appeared in the beginning of the 16th century with several theologians like Martin Luther, Ulrich Zwingli and John Calvin. At the time, these men were protesting against what they saw and heard happening inside the Roman Catholic Church. In France, the storms of persecution against the Protestants were brewing with rage, forcing them to either convert to Catholicism or to flee.

On April 30, 1598, King Henry IV signed the Edict of Nantes which finally gave the Protestant church the right to freely profess. This was not too surprising because in order for Henry IV to become king, he chose to leave the Protestant church and convert to Catholicism.

However, in the year 1685, King Louis XIV reversed this edict and the fierce persecution of Protestants resumed. During this turbulent period, the Protestants were known as Huguenots. About half a million were forced to leave France.

On the other side of the ocean where the colonists had implanted slavery, the choice was clear: Article 5 prevented Protestants from daring to challenge Catholics. So long as Protestants did nothing, allowed the system to use them, repress them, dominate them, profit from them, their place as a slave was secured.

In reality what mattered before all else for the colonists was their economic interest. Religion was the bait that allowed them to lure people and better use them. So too did the faith of the slaves in the spirit of liberty give slaves the strength to resist. If circumstances forced slaves to borrow the religion of the colonists, they were not blind:

Nguo ya kuazima haisitiri matako. Borrowed clothes cannot hide your rear end.

That is why throughout history there have always been different kinds of religion and everyone must respect all peoples' rights in this domain.

Article 6

"... Sunday must be respected ... No one has the right to force slaves to work on Sundays...."

Hypocritical Sunday

In many places, on Sundays there are slaves who rise at 2 o'clock in the morning to walk long distances to attend mass at 4 o'clock in the Catholic apostolic church, and then rush home.

Pain from the blows of batons, the lashes of whips, the cracks of sticks, and the wallops of slaps, aimed at pushing slaves toward endless work did not disappear from their memories simply because it was Sunday.

In the minds of the slaves, true rest was linked to liberty. Their natural intelligence helped them understand that liberty reigned in the souls of the faithful, like a powerful spirit sent by God.

Kucha Mungu si kilemba cheupe. Covering your head with a white turban does not mean reverence to God.

Article 7

"... The selling and purchase of slaves on Sunday and holidays is prohibited.."

A small bandage for a metastatic cancer

Slavery demonstrated that respite on Sundays and holidays was a tiny bandage on an oozing metastatic cancer. It was based on superstition dating back to the time of the ancestors of the French colonists.

These ancestors were called Franks and for a long time the Romans used them as mercenaries to fight their wars, invade territories, burn down houses and raze entire villages. There were no more ferocious bandits than them. With weapons, the Franks repeatedly proclaimed their wish to live free. To defend their territory or country that they called Francia, the Franks waged wars and organized ceremonies seeped in superstitious beliefs.

Observing one short day of respite was nothing compared to the human and animal sacrifices that the ancestors of the colonists performed to calm the various gods or spirits that they adored. The god that the Franks considered as the father of all gods was called Rotan. Both he and his wife were considered gods.

His wife was called Frigg and her role was to bestow power to either conceive or win wars and defeat enemies. These two gods, Rotan and Frigg, had a son named Thor, who was also considered to be a god.

Just as people of other countries such as Greece, Rome and Egypt, the ancestors of the French colonists adored idols, the moon and the sun. They frequently organized feasts and banquets for the dead. If there was among the deceased a Frank who was considered to be particularly courageous and fierce, a great ceremony was performed beneath a sacred tree or in a cave or on top of a mountain to crown this deceased as a god too. This is how Arminius, or Hermann, was elevated to the status of god.

These beliefs existed since time immemorial. Just as salt melts in water, these beliefs melted into religion, into tradition, into culture and into people's minds and spirits. *Tabia ni ngozi ya mwili.* Habits are like the body's skin.

When reason and intelligence blossom in the garden of religion, comprehension and great respect for the religion of all thrive and the strength of love triumphs over mystification and superstition. When, in contrast, trickery is practiced under the cover of religion, it's like using a tiny bandage, applied with an adhesive dipped in superstition, to cover a metastatic cancer. This is the technique used by cats to eat rats.

Paka akiwa hakimu panya hawezi kushinda kesi. So long as the cat is judge, the rat will never win its case.

Article 8

"... If you are not catholic, your marriage is not valid
... and your children are not legitimate ..."

Paradise for men, hell for women

The torment of the daughters of Africa always burned hotter than the ovens of hell. There were those who refused to bear children who would suffer their same fate. During the day they worked like beasts to enrich the coffers of the colonists and at night, some were made to continue to offer pleasures in the colonists' beds.

Before any consideration of marriage, the daughters of Africa, who were in the majority among the slaves, were treated like dirt during the day, but sweet mangos at night. As savage as the male colonists could be, they often fell in love with female slaves. These women drove the colonists crazy every time the colonists laid eyes on them.

Jicho halina pazia. The eye does not have a curtain.

Though they are more savage than a wild beast, or as ferocious as a leopard, large and small colonists alike know that: *Chui naye ana mke.* Even a leopard has a wife.

Having a wife is normal, but what wife and under what conditions? One slave or one white woman, if they could find one among the few whites? To prevent colonists from marrying other than white women, in 1680 France sent 250 white women to Martinique. Three years later another group of 250 was sent.

In that same year, 1683, France sent many white women prostitutes, called "girls of joy," to Quebec, Canada, to prevent marriages between white French men and indigenous Canadians.

Despite laws, racist or not, many black women bore the children of white men. In 1680 there were already approximately 350 mulattos in Barbados, 170 in Guadeloupe and 314 in Martinique. All children are children; no child chooses his father or who she wants as her mother. When a baby is born, he is innocent. So he should not be made to pay for what he neither did, can do, ask to do, help to do or refuse to do.

The question of legitimate and illegitimate children proves how the authorities never ceased to deepen the divisions of prejudice. Children that society labels as illegitimate can feel inferior compared to children that society considers as proper, legitimate children.

Slavery by itself was infused and totally infested with prejudice. Any scheme to further infect the minds of slaves with the virus of an inferiority complex yielded significant benefit to the colonists: this virus was enough to handicap the brain.

Article 9

"... *Married men who are not slaves and have children
outside the bonds of marriage must pay a fine; if a
married man has a child with a slave, neither the
child nor the mother must have contact with the father;
... if the father was not yet married, he must marry the
slave in the catholic church and the slave will be freed
and the child will be born free ...*"

A trap in hell

The contradictions that weave across article 9 make slavery resemble an oven in hell that has, at the same time, a trap. The oven of course is for the burning slave. The trap is for the colonist profiteering on the back of Africa.

Mtego bila chambo hanasi. A trap without bait will not catch anything.

This trap is baited with sacred flesh. This trap is baited with a flesh never meant to be eaten. This trap is baited with the beautiful daughters of Africa who drive the colonists mad, luring them into the racist trap that the colonists set for themselves. If the Swahili proverb says: *Vita havina macho*, war has no eyes, it seems that for racist colonists sex too had no eyes.

Article 10

*"... When a slave marries, the consent of her parents
counts for nothing; it is the consent of the master
that counts ... "*

For the white colonist every person is not a human being

Despite the indignation and humiliation of article 10 it is like a dry twig
that does not need a wind to fall from a tree. The issue of marriage is just
a gentle breeze that blows softly, an excuse to drop nonsense in a law that
is, already by itself, ludicrous.

Tawi kavu kuanguka si ajabu. It is not surprising when a dry branch falls.

After operation kidnapping the colonists clearly demonstrated through
unprecedented violence that for them, every person is not a human being.
A slave is a beast or an item possessed by the colonist. Therefore it is the
consent of the colonist — and only his — that means anything.

On this unbalanced, lopsided scale of justice the will of the colonists
weighs more than any massive boulder; the will of the slave means nothing.
When we say every person is a human being, the colonists reply not every
person is a human being.

When we say that there are no people who are more human than others:
the colonists say that is a joke! A joke to make a black man dream that
he has climbed a coconut tree, plucked a coconut, peeled the coconut
and opened it to eat just at the moment when the last of a razor-sharp
rawhide will tell him to stop dreaming.

If a few whites married a few slaves, that was not enough for anyone to
dream: there was no place in the system for "every person is a human
being." These few marriages never erased in the racist mentality that the
role of slaves was to harvest coconuts, and the role of colonists was to
eat the coconuts.

Nazi haishindani na jiwe. A ripe coconut cannot compete with a stone.

This is how the racist colonist thought because he believed that he was
superior. There was no comparison possible because in his mind the

African was inferior to the white. Regardless of marriage or other living arrangements, it was always the case of one superior being versus an inferior being.

Article 11

"...A parish priest cannot marry a slave without the
consent of his or her master ... The master does not
have the right to force the slave to marry if he refuses..."

A picometer vs. a master

The insistence of this article on the omnipotence of the slave master reduced the slave to a picometer at the master's foot. What does a picometer measure? It takes two billion picometers to equal one meter.

Moreover, this article was a double-edged sword. It reduced by a tiny fraction the authority of the slave master and added to the so-called rights of slaves — as if the slaves ever had any rights! It didn't go very far, as long as the dawn of liberty remained hidden.

Mficha uchi hazai. A woman who hides her nakedness cannot give birth.

Article 12

"... When two married slaves have a child, this child
becomes the private property of the colonist who is
the mother's master and not the colonist who is
the father's master..."

It is a crime. Period.

This article targets slaves who are married and who do not have the same master. However the real precision should be put to these two questions: who are the mother and father of this child? Are the colonists blind?

People who suffer from a disease called daltonism have problems with their eyes, which is why they cannot distinguish between the colors red and green. When colonists fail to differentiate between a child's mother and that mother's boss, their blindness exceeds any normal bounds.

It is a crime. Period. A terrible crime that condemns a tiny innocent victim to live like an animal before his mother has even delivered him. The criminal who refuses to see the difference between good and evil pretends to have the power to swim the length of an ocean. *Bahari haivukwi kwa kuogolea.* The ocean cannot be crossed by swimming.

Article 13

"*... When a free woman bears a child, the child is free even if the father is a slave; if the mother is a slave, her child is a slave even if the father is free ...*"

Different kinds of scissors...

Try as they did to wield slavery like a pair of deadly tailor's scissors it was impossible for colonists to cut from the slave mother's garment a dress for her newborn child. If mother's frock had already been reduced to tattered rags and continued to fray and shred under the slave master's whip, what kind of baby's dress could it possibly make?

Is that why colonists preferred to aim the crossing blades of *these* scissors at human flesh instead while the sun of exploitation scorched the bared backs of mothers? Were these same scissors somehow supposed to shade mothers from the flaming sun that had already burned them to a crisp?

Kivuli cha fimbo hakimfichi mtu jua. The shade from a stick does not hide a person from the sun.

For mothers and fathers who dream of a normal life for their children the solution cannot be cut using *these* scissors because the solution is liberty. Freedom for all mothers, all fathers, all children, everyone, everywhere.

Bata mtaga mayai usimchinje kwa tamaa ya wengi. Do not slaughter a duck that is hatching eggs if you want more ducks.

Article 14

*"... When a baptized slave dies, his master must bury
him in holy ground ... ; if the slave was not baptized
he must be buried at night, not far from where he died ..."*

Sham baptism, sham recompense

From birth to death there remains the issue of baptism. It's like a burning candle held upside down by the colonists to bury christened slaves in cemeteries claimed to be holy. This sham recompense was rooted in nothing more than tradition, and not in solutions.

Since time immemorial the bodies of the deceased have been respected. This is why it is not surprising that cemeteries existed before the invention of writing, about 5,300 years ago. Egyptians created underground cemeteries that they called necropoles.

After the baptism of Clovis, king of France from 481 to 511, cemeteries took on an even holier status for the Roman apostolic Catholic Church. Generally cemeteries and churches were next to one another. Persons not in good standing with the church could not be buried next to righteous believers. It is this longstanding tradition that the colonists used to arrive at article 14 as all-powerful beings holding in their hand, from its lit end, a baptismal candle. Whereas the true path to baptism is the emergence from all forms of death, toward life, the baptism of the colonists did the exact opposite: destroy life to give death.

Sacrificing the life of a slave was equal to sacrificing the life of an animal for the colonist. He bound both the christened slave and the un-christened slave to the foot of the table of slavery, where he could safely declare to both: *Chaka la simba halilali nguruwe.* A pig does not sleep in a lion's den.

Article 15

"... Slaves cannot circulate with weapons or large sticks ... "

Neither weapons nor big sticks, but ...

It was during the 9th century that the Chinese discovered how to make weapons like cannons that used gunpowder to shoot people. These weapons were used widely to fight, attack enemies and to make war. How did these weapons cross the borders to Europe?

This matter should interest all grandchildren of the victims of slavery because the colonists relied heavily on these weapons in kidnapping Africans, roping them like wild beasts, raining blows and strikes upon them, shackling them to one another to expedite them to America as slaves.

While the Chinese were making weapons such as cannons, their trade in silk was highly profitable. The Romans, for example, loved to dress in silk clothing. They were crazy about it! The importance of this commodity led the authorities of Rome to name the major route connecting the Asian, European and African continents, "the silk route"; yes, that was what it was called. It measured more than 8,000 miles.

Commodities other than silk were traded on this route. According to different sources weapons continuously traveled the silk route and crossed into Europe through to the 15th century as this trade route began to lose its importance.

Weapons also made their way to Europe during the first half of the 13th century when the Mongolians marched from China to Europe. The arrival of weapons in the country of the colonists meant death for Africa.

During the 14th century, as Arabs utilized deadly weapons to continue to invade various territories of Africa, Europeans on their side were preparing weapons, lots of weapons for their 1492 expedition that would bring slavery and death.

Article 15 prohibited slaves from bearing arms or batons. Every slave, without exception had to be cautious. *Nyumba kubwa husitiri mambo makubwa.* A big house hides big secrets.

Big secrets that conceal big worries, deep suspicions, great vigilance. Even when the rage of all the victims had not yet exploded like a bomb, the colonists could smell the anger in the bushes and on the tops of mountains. A mere twig was enough to make them tremble in their boots.

Article 16

*"... Slaves belonging to different masters are forbidden
from gathering together both during the day and at night ... "*

Divide to subjugate

The same concerns were addressed here in article 16. The sheer possibility that slaves could unify terrified the colonists. Once 2 or 3 victims assembled, the colonists, knowing how wrong they were, became suspicious. This is why they saw conspiracies to overthrow slavery under every rock.

In truth, both the victims and their tormentors were sitting on a bomb. Neither fully understood that the spark of unity was enough to make the situation explode. From the womb of Africa the victims had learned a beautiful lesson: A single finger cannot eat okra, nor can one hand applaud.

You don't have to go to school to understand the importance of these proverbs:
Elimu maisha si vitabu. Education is life, not books. Education comes from life itself, not from books. *Akili ni mali.* Knowledge is wealth.

Every page from the big book of life has the word *unity* written on it. This is where victims learned another beautiful lesson on the intelligence of frogs: If a mere frog knows that the only way to kill an elephant is to enter its trunk, imagine the intelligence gained by people who are united.

Chura huweza kumwua tembo. A frog can kill an elephant.

To laud this intelligence, the book of life adds:
Akili ni nywele, kila mtu ana zake. Intelligence is like hair,
everyone has their own type.

Poetry

Article 17

*"... Slave masters who allow slaves with different owners
to assemble must be fined ..."*

10 cent fine!

What fine? Where does the money come from?
Is it not still the sweat and blood of the slaves?

If there is a 10 cent fine paid
The colonist is prepared
To extract 10 times more work and energy from the slave
Who, thankfully never forgot that:
Fimbo ya mbali haiuwi nyoka.
A stick that remains at a distance will not kill a snake.

Article 18

"... No slave must ever sell sugar cane, for whatever
reason or occasion, even with the permission of their master ... "

Bitter as wormwood

As sweet as sugar is in the mouths of the colonists,
It is as bitter as wormwood in the mouths of slaves
Who struggle to plant the sugar canes, cut the sugar canes,
Mill the sugar canes, never daring to
Take a chance to sell a tiny piece of that sugar cane.

As sweet as sugar is in the mouths of the colonists,
It is as bitter as wormwood in the mouths of slaves.
As sweet as sugar is in the mouths of the colonists,
In the mouth of slaves, who struggle to plant sugar cane,
It is still the sharp shavings of the sugar cane, crawling with ants.

If tragedy cannot be forewarned,
Shida haina hodi,
Trouble does not knock on the door,
Sugar cane was a great tragedy
That sounded its warning
At the start of slavery.

A great tragedy that from the start
Lined the pockets of the colonists with riches.
A great tragedy that made slaves sing
Low and deep in their hearts:

Mchuma juani hula kivulini.
One who harvests in the sun eats in the shade.
Mpanda ngazi hushuka.
When you climb up a ladder you must also climb down.

Leo kwako, kesho kwa mwenzio.
Today is for you, tomorrow is for your friend.
Haba na haba hujaza kibaba.
Little by little fills the measure.

Mchuma juani hula kivulini.
One who harvests in the sun eats in the shade.
Leo kwako, kesho kwa mwenzio.
Today is for you, tomorrow is for your friend.

Article 19

*"... Slaves are forbidden from selling any type of
commodities, even fruit, vegetables, firewood, grains
for cooking and for animals without the express
permission of their master ... "*

Sugar cane spoils twins

When it comes to commodities such as fruits, vegetables, firewood,
Grains for animal feed, the master must grant his permission
For the slave to sell them at the market.
When it comes to sugar cane, not so, according to article 18.

No slave has the right to sell sugar cane. Period.
Why was sugar cane so important?
Why was it so valuable?
Was our country's umbilical cord cut with a sugar cane?

Sugar cane may have originated from
One of the world's largest islands, New Guinea.
Only Australia and Greenland are any bigger.
Once upon a time sugar cane grew like weeds in New Guinea.

Indo China is another ancestral home of sugar cane
Where, too, it grew in great abundance.
Roughly 6 centuries before the birth of Christ,
The Chinese were harvesting sugar cane in their fields.

In the 8th century when the Arabs were all-powerful,
They brought sugar cane to Spain for the first time.
This is why Christopher Columbus was able
To arrive with the plant when he landed on our home shores
During his second voyage in 1493.

Whether or not the plant was already in the country,
One thing is certain, with Columbus's arrival
Sugar cane was transformed into a powerful twin weapon
Simultaneously bringing life to the colonists
And death to the slaves.

Ng'ombe wa maskini hazai mapacha.
A poor man's cow does not give birth to twins.
Yet the sugar cane of the all-powerful gives birth to foul twins.

Article 20

*"… There must be two regulators in every market
to control the foods and commodities that the slaves bring …"*

Control

Control below, control in the center,
Control above. Everywhere, 2 regulators
Arrived to control the markets.

This type of control manifested, among other things,
The vigilance of the white colonists who seemed to be saying:

Usipoziba ufa, utajenga ukuta.
If you do not fill a crack, you will build a wall.

However the wall of slavery
Had been erected long ago.
The more the regulators controlled
The more the slaves decided to destroy
Both the wall and the owners of that wall.

Article 21

*"... Seize all that the slaves bought if they did
not have the permission of their masters ..."*

And? And nothing!

And? What else could the colonist seize
After seizing the liberty of the Africans?
Food? Commodities? And? And nothing.
Because for the victims liberty was all.

Seizing a people's liberty is one thing
Seizing the spirit of that liberty is another.
As long as the spirit of liberty is alive,
There will always be a good fight
To recapture liberty.

Mfa maji haishi kutapatapa.
One who is drowning does not stop struggling.

Article 22

*"... Every week, the slave master must give every slave that
is 10 years old or more 2 and a half pots of manioc flour,
according to measures used in Paris, or else 3 cassavas that
each weigh at least 2 and a half pounds ... and 2 pounds of
salted beef or else 3 pounds of fish...*

As for infants, once they are weaned and until the age of 10,
they will be given half of the quantity of food indicated in
article 22, every week ..."

Legitimate self-defense

If I were not a new born baby,
Boy, would I talk to the white colonist
To tell him what is in my heart!

If I were not a new born baby,
I would start talking in the morning
All the way into the night, in the ears of the white colonist.

If I were not a new born baby,
I would speak clearer, louder and more
To tell the white colonist, you are crazy!

You ate my father without chewing him,
You ate my mother without salt
And now you are out to eat me without even cooking me.

Wait! What is this business of measuring food out
In tiny begging bowls
So as not to die of starvation?

Ah, Mister white colonist,
Even animals must eat well
So as not to die.

Farasi hamuwawezi, tembo mtawalishani?
If you cannot feed a horse, how are you going to feed an elephant?

Ah, Mister white colonist,
If you cannot allow me to eat with dignity,
How can I not claim legitimate defense?

Article 23

"... slaves cannot be given sugar cane juice in the
place of food indicated in article 22 ..."

Sugar cane is our blood

Sugar cane juice deceives white colonists
But it does not deceive us,
Black men and women of Africa.
Sugar cane juice is sugar cane and the cane is our blood.

To deceive a cat the rat
Offers the cat rice instead of sugar cane.
Because the cat understands it says:
Paka hashibi kwa wali, matilabaye ni panya.
A cat is not satisfied with rice it wants the rat.

Sugar cane juice deceives white colonists
But it does not deceive us,
Black men and women of Africa.
Sugar cane juice is sugar cane and the cane is our blood.

For a cat to catch a rat
It offers it a trap instead of sugar cane.
Because the rat understands it says:
Mla mbuzi hulipa ng'ombe.
One who eats a goat will repay with a cow.

Sugar cane juice deceives white colonists
But it does not deceive us,
Black men and women of Africa.
Sugar cane juice is sugar cane and the cane is our blood.

Because the cat knows, the rat knows,
Neither rice, the trap, nor the sugar cane will remain.
Because the cat knows, the rat knows,
Neither rice, the trap, nor the sugar cane will remain.

The colonist wants to devour the slave
Like the cat devours the rat
But what the colonist doesn't know
Is that it is black men and women who make sugar cane
And not the sugar cane that makes the children of Africa.
Sugar cane is sugar cane, sugar cane is our blood.

The colonists want to devour the slaves
Like the cat devours the rat
But what the colonists don't know is that
Since their days in Guinea
Proud Africans swore to drink
The soup of justice from a pot of dignity
Boiled on 3 rock-fires called
Liberty—Equality—Fraternity.

Ah, Mister white colonist,
Sugar cane is sugar cane, sugar cane is not your blood.
Sugar cane is sugar cane, sugar cane is our blood.

Article 24

*"... slave masters cannot offer slaves the possibility to earn
money during the week in exchange for giving them food ... "*

Learn to understand

The rope tied around the slave's neck was already tight
article 24 adds another knot.
Every word from the white colonist's mouth
Is another knot that tightens the noose.

Lililo moyoni ulimi huiba.
The tongue steals what is in the heart.

Could the victims understand
The intentions of the colonists?
Yes, they did. They heard and saw much.

Hearing and seeing is one thing, understanding is another.
Learning to understand is still another because truly,
In the process of learning to understand,
The human who has been enslaved cannot sit and wait in vain.

Thankfully this wisdom shone in the spirit,
Minds, eyes, entrails, blood
And deep recesses of the hearts of the grandchildren of Africa.

Heri kufa macho kuliko kufa moyo.
Better the death of the eye than the death of the spirit.

Article 25

"... Every year every slave master must give
his slave 2 items of clothing or 4 yards of fabric ..."

The skin of our backs, backsides, breasts, bodies ...

It's true that since we were small babies
Nursing at our mothers' breasts
We heard our elders say:
Afya ni bora kuliko mali.
Health is better than wealth.

But how can we have health
If we are forced to dress in old rags,
That make us look like derelicts attracting curses?

It's true that since we were small babies
Nursing at our mothers' breasts,
We heard our elders say:
Kazi mbaya siyo mchezo mzuri.
Bad labor is not a fair game; there is no dishonorable work.

But how can we work
If we don't have our health?
And how can we have our health
If we have to dress in old rags,
That make us look like derelicts attracting curses?

With only two old rags allotted for the year
If we don't walk naked,
One hand covering our front
The other our back, it's not the colonist's fault.

It's true that since we were small babies
Nursing at our mothers' breasts
We heard our elders say:

Mpofu hasahau mkongojo wake.
A blind person doesn't forget his cane.

But we always forget
Our clothing before heading off to work
Because our shirt is the skin of our back,
The pants we wear, the skin of our backside,
The pretty brassieres that we wear to go out,
The skin of our breasts,
The pretty dresses that we lounge in,
The skin of our bodies.

Because our most private parts are in the front
The small bit of cloth is for the front.
As for the back, we'll ask to borrow.
Though since we were small babies
Nursing at our mothers' breasts,
We heard our elders say:
Nguo ya kuazima haisitiri matako.
Borrowed clothes don't cover your rear.

Article 26

*"… Slaves who are not fed, clothed and taken care
of by their masters can bring their master to court …"*

Stop telling lies!

Colonist, if you dared say that you gave slaves justice
Know that, with the respect that I owe you,
I must say, that you speak with a forked tongue!
A pointed, sharp tongue able to dig holes of lies.
The hole of a lie dug with a sharp tongue is always wide.

Shimo la ulimi mkono halifukiki.
The hand cannot cover a hole dug by the tongue.

Colonist, if you dared say that you gave slaves justice,
Know that, with the respect that I owe you,
I must say that you speak with a forked tongue!

A pointed, sharp tongue able to dig holes of lies.
The hole of a lie dug with a sharp tongue is always shallow.

Njia wongo fupi.
The path of a lie is short; the hole of a lie is not deep.

Colonist, when you promise justice
The victim's ears hear you because
Sikio halilali na njaa
The ear never goes to sleep hungry.

Colonist, with all the respect that I owe you, stop!
Stop telling lies! Stop telling lies!

Article 27

*"... Slaves who are infirm due to age, illness or other reason,
whether the illness is curable or not, shall be nourished and
cared for by their masters. In the case that they be abandoned,
said slaves shall be awarded to the hospital ... "*

Illness

Illness is a notorious bandit:
Its greatest enemy is health,
Its strongest partner death.

As soon as illness spots medicine
The hairs on its back stand up straight.
If its eyes land on a pharmacy
It turns white with anger.

Illness is a notorious bandit:
Its greatest enemy is health,
Its strongest partner death.

Illness is known to attack with rage
Even a tiny, miniscule ant.
To treat its teeth the ant consults a dentist.
For a stomachache, the ant gets an x-ray.

Ants don't take illness lightly
Because they know that
Illness is a notorious bandit:
Its greatest enemy is health,
Its strongest partner is death.

As for me, if I had a choice
Between illness and death
Truly, I would resign myself and choose death,
An easier fate for the slave than illness.

Illness for a slave is a river of suffering
That flows to the sea of death.

Bahari iliko ndiko mito iendako.
Rivers flow to the closest sea.

Illness for a slave and the sea of death
Are the same because
Illness is a notorious bandit:
Its greatest enemy is health,
Its strongest partner is death,
Its greatest source is the colonists.

Article 28

"... *A slave does not have the right to any personal
possessions, all that he has belongs to his master* ..."

Tell me about that brother!

When a poor person works as a sharecropper
The harvest is divided, half and half.
It is an arrangement that is a distant cousin of slavery,
But a deal is a deal.

The harvest becomes a bridge of interest
Between the owner of the land

And the person who works the land.
Their mutual interest is tied to the same bridge,
Notwithstanding the prejudice that separates the two.

Daraja ukilibomoa ujue kuogolea.
If you destroy the bridge, you'd better know how to swim.

What a profound idea for thinking people!
But since when did white colonists think like this
When their teeth were sunk into slaves, ready to consume,
Devour, destroy from A to Z?

For all colonists thinking with empty brains
Slaves were nothing, slaves should have nothing.
For all colonists thinking with empty brains
Slaves were nothing, slaves should have nothing

Tell me about that brother! But don't forget!
Siku ya kufa nyani miti yote huteleza.
The day a monkey is destined to die, all trees are slippery.

Article 29

*"... If a slave master goes bankrupt in his business,
he owes the slave nothing ..."*

What, you think that I don't see!

What! You think that I don't see! Oh, my goodness!
Well, I would have to be crazy not to see that
You saddle me, bridle me, mount me, ride me
To profit while I sacrifice.

My ears are sharp but they never heard
So much as a small thank you
Escape from the mouth
Of a person who doesn't consider me even like a dog.
Today my nose is clogged but not from flu.

My goodness! How could I not see?
Well, I would have to be crazy not to see
You saddle me, bridle me, mount me, ride me
To profit while I sacrifice.

This sacrifice clogs my nose with wads of cotton of patience
But it does not cover my eyes to this injustice.
There are 5 lessons to be learned from this patience
One for each finger:

1
Bandu bandu, humaliza gogo.
Little by little the log will be chopped.

2
Kibuzi na kibuzi hununua jahazi.
Small goat by small goat, a ship is purchased.

3
Simba mwenda pole ndiye mla nyama.
The lion that goes slowly/cautiously eats meat.

4
Ondoa dari uezeke paa.
Remove the ceiling to thatch the roof.

5
Daraja livuke ulifikiapo.
Cross the bridge when you reach it.
Therefore, that day, we will surely arrive there.
Because that bridge is the bridge of liberty.

Article 30

*"... Slaves cannot work for the state ... slaves cannot
be witnesses in court ... slaves can only work with
their masters ..."*

Article 31

"... *A slave accused of a crime cannot appear in court, his master must appear for him ...*"

Article 32

"... *A slave master is not responsible for crimes committed by his slave ...*"

Articles 33, 34, 35, 38

These articles allow a slave to be condemned to death. Slaves can be sentenced to death:

"... *If a slave has struck his master in the face or has drawn blood, or has similarly struck the wife of his master, his mistress, or their children ...* " *(Article 33)*

"... *If a slave has a conflict with a person who is not a slave, depending on the gravity of the conflict ...*" *(Article 34)*

"... *If a slave steals a horse, millet, cow ... depending on the gravity of the theft ...*" *(Article 35)*

"... *If a slave escapes for a third time ...*" *(Article 38)*

That day! Ahh!

Before the law can even condemn me
I carry my coffin in my arms.
The rope that will hang me, hangs from my neck,
The hole that will bury me has already been dug.

Who made the coffin? I did.
Who tied the cord's knot? I did.
Who dug the hole? I did.

Sir death, the bell is in your hand.
As soon as you ring it

I will respond, present! I am here!
An innocent person who is courageous
Is not afraid of death.

After all the blows from sticks, the kicks,
The hurled chairs that you lashed at me
And were enough to kill me,
If the spirit of *mondong* possessed me only to
Threaten legitimate self-defense I was as good as dead.

You curse and say that you will kill me.
Well, what are you waiting for?
Yes, what are you waiting for?

After all that I suffered because I escaped
Once, then twice,
You declare that if I escape a third time
You will kill me.
Well, what are you waiting for?
Yes, what are you waiting for?

Before the law can even condemn me,
I carry my coffin in my arms.
The rope that will hang me, hangs from my neck,
The hole that will bury me has already been dug.

Who made the coffin? I did.
Who tied the cord's knot? I did.
Who dug the hole? I did.

Sir death, the bell is in your hand,
As soon as you ring it
I will respond, present! I am here!
An innocent person who is courageous
Is not afraid of death.

Since the horrid kidnapping operation was unleashed
The white colonist killed my father,
He killed my mother, he killed my sister,
He killed my brother, he killed my family
Without the law ever asking, with what right?

Today, it is for these same colonists
That the law condemns victims
Who are pressing
Day and night, all the time and
    everywere
For justice and freedom.
Everywhere, all the time, all day, even at night.

This law is the curtain that criminals borrow
To hide the faces of villains behind suits and ties.
This law is the flag that assassins raise
To praise thugs.
This law is the red carpet that the colonists use
To soak the blood of the innocent, flowing
Everywhere, all day and all night.

This river of blood does not stop them from taunting us!
Look at how they laugh, laugh without stopping!
But a time will come.

Kuni ya juu uchaga hucheka iliyo motoni.
Logs on the top of the wood pile laugh at the wood in the fire.

When the gas of our anger is poured onto the fire of slavery
Nothing will be able to extinguish this raging fire.
All the fires in the sugar cane fields
Are an exercise for this fire of justice.

When the gas of our anger is poured onto the fires of slavery
Nothing will be able to extinguish this raging fire.
All the fires in the sugar cane fields
Are practice for this fire of justice.

That day, that day! Ahh! Sorry for the colonists!
Justice will triumph!
That day, that day! Ahh! Sorry for the colonists!
Freedom will overcome!

Article 36

*"... If a slave steals a sheep, or goat, pig, chicken,
sugar cane, beans, millet, or other legume, the judge*

can punish him with a lashing or can brand him with
a fleur de lys ... "

If anyone is to be branded ...

So that hunger doesn't end up exploding my entrails
I accept to suck on a piece of sugar cane.
Oh! Blows to the face threatens to unhinge my jaw.

Who toiled to plant the sugar cane?
Who labored to till, water and weed the fields?
Who bled while cutting, lifting,
Carrying, peeling, milling, pulverizing,
Mixing the sugar cane to make syrup,
Sugar, molasses, sweets, rum, etc.?

Me. Yes me, indeed.
You are ranting about a tiny splinter of sugar cane.
God! Look at how you have made me vomit blood!
Look at how my two ears are urinating blood!

Despite that, your sizzling branding iron
Is already in your hand,
Ready to brand me like they brand a horse.
May lightning strike me,
Today it will not go down like this!

Even if my grandmother always told me
Heri kujikwaa kidole kuliko kujikwaa ulimi.
Better to stumble over your toe
Than to stumble over your tongue,
Today, I am damn tired, I can't take it anymore.

I can die, but I won't die suffocating.
And if I don't scream, I will suffocate.
Yes, I must scream stop the thief! Help!
For God's sake! Stop!
For goodness sake, help me scream no!
No! For God's sake! Stop the thief!

If there is a thief, you are the damn thief.

You, the white colonist who robbed
My entire race, all my possessions, my liberty.
Today, if anyone is to be branded
I have decided to brand you
Over your entire body
Because your entire body reads thief.

Article 37

"... In addition to the blows that a slave may receive for
a theft or for any other infraction committed against a
non-slave, his master is obliged to make reparations to
the offended party or risk losing the slave to that person
... the master has 3 days to decide ..."

Article 38

"... A slave who has been on the run for one month from
the day his master reported him to the police, shall have
his ears cut off and shall be branded with a fleur de lys
on one shoulder. If he commits the same infraction for
another month, again counting from the day he is reported,
he shall have his hamstring cut and be branded with a
fleur de lys on the other shoulder. The third time,
he shall be put to death."

The scissors of legitimate self-defense

Condemning the small ant for hiding
Inside a coconut while it takes a needed break
Is popular in the courts here.

Cutting the ant's ears and its hamstring
To mix with the fleshly inside of the coconut
To feed to the dogs,
Is what is popular in the courts here.

Maji ya kifuu bahari ya chungu.
The water in a coconut is an ocean to an ant.

It's the same thing for runaway slaves!
Don't ask me where my left ear went,
Don't ask me where my right ear went.
Where could they go?
They didn't up and escape.

It's the whites who cut them off!
The tip of my ear went flying,
I screamed like hell!
The white said: shut your mouth!
If you yell, I'll make you eat your ears.

Another time, the white was even angrier
When he aimed the machete at my left hamstring.
The more I screamed, the more stabs to the leg
Until the hamstring loosened
And fell to the ground in a river of blood.

I fainted, awakened, fainted, awakened,
I got up, fell over and got up,
Then fell back down to the ground
Shaking like a chicken in the throes of death.
Pain, agony, suffering! The white could not care less.

The wings of the white man's ear are longer than his head.
He filled them with mud so as not to hear my howls.
At night he poured cement into his ears
So that even a mosquito
Would not disturb him with my entreaties.

It's a pity, at night the pain doesn't let me sleep.
As soon as my eyes close I know what dream will come:
That God is angry
And that he cuts both hamstrings of the white man,
As well as his ears
With a pair of scissors labeled legitimate self-defense.
Wow! I'm sure that the white would like to cut off my head
So that I can never, never dream of legitimate self-defense.

Article 44

"... We decree that slaves are property (furniture) ... "

Slaves are furniture!

Slaves are furniture! Okay! You said it, it is done!
I heard it, it's done. Slaves are furniture!

When you want to sit, you sit on me.
When you want to lie down, you lie down on me.
To buy me, you go to the market;
You sell me with no qualms
Because you have openly declared
That slaves are furniture.

Now wait! Doesn't your mouth tremble?
Do you understand the meaning of your statement?
Can it be that you are even worse than what I thought?
Seems that it was for you that it is said:

Kumwashia taa kipofu ni kuharibu mafuta.
Lighting a lantern for a blind person is a waste of kerosene.

Wait, wait, this is worse, stranger:
Even flies and trash declare that slaves are furniture.
There is no difference between slaves and furniture
Both indeed are the same.

Oh oh! Fly, you say that I am a piece of furniture,
Be careful, don't land on me! Shoo fly, shoo!
Flies can't touch clean furniture!

You too trash, pile of trash,
You say that I am a piece of furniture,
Be careful, don't touch me! Get away, away!
A pile of trash can't sit on clean furniture.

Yes, to you who say that slaves are furniture
And to you flies, trash or piles of trash
I say: go away, away!

My upbringing doesn't allow me to tell you what I want to tell you.
Go away! Go and ask your mother to explain what I mean.

Article 55

"... *Once the owner of a slave turns 25, he has
the right to free his slave so that the slave can
become a freedman ...*"

Mental slave

(No. 1)

Ajabu ya shingo kukataa kulala kitandani.
It would be strange for the neck to refuse to lie down on the bed.

It is only natural for the neck to follow the head and body.
So too, people and liberty should always be inseparable.
Once a slave gains the rights of the freedman
He is joyful, his life changes, at last he sees liberty.
However, reality shows that there are freedmen
And then there are freedmen.
There are freedmen who are free
And freedmen who are crooked.

Freedmen who are free are unshackled by the limitations
Drawn by white colonists
In their racist books with prejudicial pens.
The power of liberty, equality and fraternity runs in their veins.
The freedman is not less than the white
And not more than the slave.
Because all people are human beings,
No one is more human than the other.

However freedmen who are free
Are the opposite of freedmen who are crooked.
When the crooked freedman looks at the white he feels inferior.
As soon as he is before a child of Africa he feels superior.
The weight of prejudice piled on top of his head
Is so heavy that the brain buckles and becomes crooked.
This is a real danger! It is a potential source of a major identity crisis.

This identity crisis can lead to pathological behavior
Morning, noon and night.
When superiority and inferiority complexes collide
The consequences are enough
To damage a person for life.
The pathologies provoked by these complexes
Corrode the character like a strong acid.
Whites use these types of freedmen as sycophants,
Hired hands, spies, *restavèks,* lackeys, puppets, mental slaves.

Client presidents, mental slaves?
There are plenty!
Puppet politicians, mental slaves?
There are even more!
Lackey bourgeoisie, mental slaves?
Even more!
Lackey church officials, mental slaves?
They are everywhere!
Lackey, pretentious twit, mental slaves?
You cannot count them!
The mental slave's back is hunched
From bending before the colonist.
The badge on his shoulder reads: I, house slave.
When he stands guard before the colonist's house,
No person dares to approach.

If a child of a slave comes too close
The house slave or mental slave warns him:
Jogoo wa shamba haiwiki mjini.
The rooster from the country does not crow in the city.

If the child of a slave insists on entering the yard,
The house slave or mental slave tells him no!
Ziba mwanya usipite panya.
Fill up the cracks so that the rat cannot pass.

Where do you get off bothering people all the way here?
Afadhali mchawi kuliko mfitini.
Better a witch doctor than a troublemaker.

What do you think you are? You?!

Moto hauzai moto, huzaa jivu.
Firewood doesn't beget firewood, it begets ashes.

I see you trying to suck up to people!
Mtegemea nundu haachi kunona.
One who lives on rich food gets fat.

Get away! Go! Remove yourself from here!
Chui hakumbatiwi.
You can't hug a leopard.

Moreover you know full well that the white doesn't have
Anything for your kind of slave!
Mkono mtupu haulambwi.
One doesn't lick an empty hand.

Oh! You have spoiled my mood.
The proverb is right:
Hakuna masika yasiyokuwa na mbu.
There is no rainy season without mosquitoes.

Give me peace! Don't come and bother me today!
My only dream is to kiss the hand of the white.
Mkono usioweza kuukata, ubusu.
Kiss the hand that you cannot cut.

As if the white would ever give the mental slave that chance.
If there is anything to kiss
The lackey will only get to kiss the white man's foot.
Whenever two house slaves get drunk with
The wine of flattery they start to fight
And the colonists say:

Watetea ndizi mgomba si wao.
They argue over the bananas
But the banana tree belongs to someone else.

Boy, are these lackeys faithful!
They should be the ones that we use,
Even if the proverb always says:
Epuka wakusifuo siku zote.

Avoid those who constantly praise you.

Mental slave

(No. 2)

The child of a *slave*, the grandchild of a *slave*, that is normal.
The great grandchild of a *slave*, that is more than normal.
The great-great grandchild of a *slave*, that is still normal.
The great tragedy that all descendants of Africa must avoid
Is crawling on the ground, prostrate, like a mental slave,
Walking on bended knee, like a mental slave.
Cringing and bowing, stooped,
With no dignity, like a mental slave.

If I were the sky I would make of the rainbow,
A crown for all the descendants of slaves
Who possess character.
If I were the moon I would help mental slaves
Plant their feet firmly on the ground
And embrace the beautiful star of dignity.

If I were a needle and thread,
What beautiful dresses and robes of unity
I would sew to offer people who are mental slaves.
If I were a sewing machine I would stitch
These robes of unity in no time, free of charge.

Umoja ni nguvu, utengano ni udhaifu.
Unity is strength, division is weakness.

If I were honey I would only make syrup of understanding
To offer to all my brothers and sisters who are mental slaves.
As sweet as a chicken feather gently twirled in your ear,
It cannot be sweeter than this syrup of understanding.

Apendaye asali, huumwa na nyuki.
If you like honey, you must suffer the bees' stings.

The child of a *slave*, the grandchild of a *slave*, that is normal.
The great grandchild of a *slave*, that is more than normal.

The great-great grandchild of a *slave,* that is still normal.
The great tragedy that all descendants of Africa must avoid
Is crawling on the ground, prostrate, like a mental slave,
Walking on bended knee, like a mental slave.
Cringing and bowing, stooped,
With no dignity, like a mental slave.

If I were the ocean I would turn salt water into fresh water
To water the front doors of all who are not mental slaves.
If I were the sun I would not set until
Mental slaves straightened their backs
To walk with heads held high.

If I were a shoe I would never cover the foot of a sycophant.
If I were a shoe I would tie my laces very tight,
To avoid the heavy winds of anger from
Flinging me at the mouths of white colonists:
The white colonist drags too many mental slaves
Behind him like an old disheveled slipper.

Kasumba ya kikoloni **or mental slave**

(No. 3)

Maji ukiyavulia nguo huna budi kuyaoga.
Once you have striped off your clothes by the water you have
No other choice but to bathe.

Before the thunder of kidnapping began growling,
We, sons and daughters of Africa,
Had already undressed before the waters of liberty.
Nothing, nothing would have prevented us from
Diving and bathing in the waters of liberty.

The kidnapping of Toussaint Louverture in 1803
Was a comma, not a period
In the history book of Haiti that is filled with love.

Love of liberty, love of liberty with no reserve!
Love that made Toussaint Louverture passionate for liberty,
To the point that he sacrificed his whole life

To break the chains of slavery.
Love that made Papa Dessalines stand,
Head held high, to declare:
Forward! Let us go! Forward! Liberty or death!

Love that makes us, sons and daughters of Haiti,
Swear to never be a *kasumba ya kikoloni*
A *kasumba ya kikoloni* equals a mental slave.

If Toussaint Louverture was a *kasumba ya kikoloni*,
The flag of Haiti would never be raised as the flag
Of the first Black peoples in the world to take their independence.

If Papa Dessalines was a *kasumba ya kikoloni*,
Haiti would not have honored either Africa or humanity
When it declared that we are free as of the 1 January 1804.

Praise for our Ancestors! Honor and respect for them!
The more the sun of love unceasingly warms us,
Continuing to dampen us with the perspiration of dignity,
The more we swear to never be a *kasumba ya kikoloni*.

Kasumba ya kikoloni always has a begging bowl
In each hand ready to plead for a piece of liberty.
As if they ever gifted this to the sons and daughters of Africa!
Liberty is never given, it is taken.

What the colonists give freely is misery.
Free misery to darken any tenebrous blackout.
A blackout that causes the blind and the *kasumba ya kikoloni*
To claim that laziness and slothfulness
Are the twin causes of the misery of Blacks.

Ahchum! Ahchum! If I don't sneeze
Ahchum! Ahchum, this lie will strangle me!
No doubt, you too, you must sneeze
Ahchum! Ahchum to avoid this lie.

Misery is the alter ego of slavery
The two are the two sides of the same coin.
Birds of the same feather.

Neither just happened.
Neither simply fell out of the sky from nowhere.
White colonists stand accused of neither.

All of us who are victims have our responsibility.
But today's misery is a direct consequence of
400 years of slavery that, like it or not, must impel
Reparation, restitution, reparation, restitution.

In order for the butcher to succeed in mounting this nefarious
    conspiracy,
Whites unified across social lines:

Meno ya mbwa hayaumani.
The dog's teeth do not bite one another.
Especially when they join to bite, with rage and to the bone,
The sons and daughters of Africa.

What, luckily for us, the butchers did not see,
Was our own mile-high wall of unity!
Mpiga ngumi ukuta huumiza mkonowe.
One who boxes with a wall hurts his hand.

What, luckily for us, the butchers did not know
Is our beautiful philosophy and lessons of wisdom that provide:
Ndege mjanja hunaswa kwa tundu bovu.
Even the clever bird gets caught in a worthless trap.

What, unfortunately for them, the butchers did not want to recognize,
Is that we too are human beings and therefore:
Adui ya mtu ni mtu.
The enemy of a person is a person.

What the butchers could never admit is that
We victims always refused
To beg for charity because, firstly, we have dignity
And secondly we understood long ago that:
Ombaomba huleta unyonge.
Continuous begging leads to poverty/misery.

What, luckily for us, the butchers did not grasp,

Is that we who are victim of all sorts of crime,
Would never have trusted them, not one millimeter.
A cat burned in hot water is afraid when it sees cold water.

Mtafunwa na nyoka akiona unyasi hushtuka.
One who has been bitten by a snake startles at a reed.

What, luckily for us, the butchers could not learn,
Was the need to abandon the arrogance that blinded them
That caused them to confuse a fisherman and a pirate.
One should never mistake the two.

Mvuvi ndiye ajuaye pweza alipo.
It is the fisherman who knows where to find the cuttlefish.

As for us, the victims, we knew
Not to cover our eyes with this mask of arrogance.
On the weapons front the butchers surpassed us.
On the people front we beat them at the start.
And it was at this intersection that we waited for them
At the last rendezvous, the rendezvous of victory
In Vertières, November 18, 1803.

Like any good garden hoe we know where our strength lies.
Imara ya jembe kaingoje shamba.
The power of the hoe sits in the garden.

A garden that we have been tilling
Since our days in the bowels of Africa.
A garden of liberty that we promised to water
With both our sweat and the blood flowing in our veins.

Ahadi ni deni.
A promise is a debt.

It is the harvest indeed that we celebrated in the name of Dessalines
In the city of Gonaives, the 1st of January 1804.
To celebrate this harvest of independence,
The sons and daughters of Africa
Kept their eyes wide open, always.

Intelligent sons and daughters of Africa do not mistake
A lie, disguised as a piece of cheese, for the moon of liberty.
Intelligent sons and daughters of Africa do not discard
Their old pots from Africa
For shiny new pots from white colonists.

Usiache mbachao kwa msala upitao.
Don't give up your old prayer rug.

Courageous sons and daughters of Africa look behind
Look in front to see where you have come from,
Where you are going while you declare:
Iliyopita si ndwele, ganga ijayo.
That which has already passed is not a sickness;
Heal that which shall come.

Healing for our future requires for
All *kasumba ya kikoloni*
A vaccination to their consciences.
Yes, a powerful vaccination to their consciences
So that we can unblock the road to
Reparation—Restitution.

Healing for our future requires that
All *kasumba ya kikoloni*
Find a powerful serum of dignity,
A good vitamin of fraternity
So that we can all stand together
Walk together and create together
One *vèvè*,[3] not two, just one;
A *vèvè* traced with a flour of
Liberty, Equality and Fraternity.

And the flour of this *vèvè* has
Only one color, not two, only one,
Only one color, that most beautiful of colors
Because it is the color of love.

---

3. A design/symbol traced on the ground using flour; it has a specific significance in African cultures

Love for all,
Black or white;
Rich or poor, the weak or the strong
Who want us to stand together,
Walk together and build together
A new society where at last,
At long last, misery will be put in a museum
While a civilization of love will shine.

D) *Kama* Haïti ?
Like Haïti ?

Ingekuwa muhimu sana kutambua kama kuna maneno katika Kikreyòl ambayo
mizizi yake inatoka kwenye lugha ya Kiswahili kama Haïti. Kwa hakika
tunaweza kusema kuna maneno yanayoonyesha uhusiano na Kiswahili au
lugha ya kibantu. Lakini maneno haya siyo mengi. Katika orodha ifuatayo,
tutagundua maneno ya Kikreyòl ambayo yanatoka katika lugha ya Kiswahili
na maneno mengine ambayo tungetumia kufanya "mnemonics" kama tuna-
taka kujifunza maneno mwengine. Hilo lingekuwa jambo la kuvutia kwa
watu wengine kwa sababu shamba la lugha hii inaonyesha mila ya watoto
na madhuria ya Afrika.

It would be very important to discover if, like the word Haiti, there are
other words in Kreyòl with roots from Swahili. Surely, we say, there are
words that indicate a relationship with Swahili or the Bantu languages. But
these words are few. In the following list we will discover words in Kreyòl
that come from Swahili and other words that we can use as mnemonics
if we want to learn new vocabulary. It may also appear interesting for
some people because this linguistic field reflects the culture of the sons,
daughters, and descendants of Africa.

Swahili and Kreyòl words for mnemonics or linguistic roots

1. **Baraka**   blessing *(benediksyon)*[4]

   Inahitaji akili na baraka ku kuwa "barak."
   It requires intelligence and blessing to be a "barak."
   Fòk yon <u>barak</u>[5] gen intelijans ak benediksyon.

---

4. The words in parentheses are the Kreyòl translation of the Swahili words.
5. Compare the underlined Kreyòl word with the Swahili.

2. Chakula food *(manje)*

Kwetu, "chaka" ni chakula.[6]
In our country "tchaka" is a food.
Lakay, tchaka se manje.

3. -Chupa[7] bottle; to move quickly; to jump on *(kouri vit; sote sou)*

Gari inachupa kwa haraka katika mashimo.
The car falls in and out of the holes.
Machinn nan rantre tchoup tchoup nan twou yo.

4. Dakiza to interrupt; to contradict *(entèwonp; kontredi)*

Wakati ahutaki kuzungumza kwa moyo mweupe, unazungumza kwakujidakiza.
When you don't want to speak clearly you speak in code.
Lè w pa vle pale aklè, ou pale an daki.

Wamejificha kwenye mahandaki.[8]
They hide in the tunnels.
Yo kache nan tinèl yo.

**Hawawezi kuzungumza kikawaida
kwasababu wanazungumza kwenye mahandaki.**
They can't speak normally that's why they speak in code.
Yo pa ka pale nòmalman, se pou sa yo pale andaki.

5. Fofofo soundly *(pwofondeman; fonfonfon)*

Analala fofofo.[9]
He sleeps soundly.
Li dòmi fonfonfon.

6. Futa kufuta erase; to cancel *(efase)*

---

6. In Swahili **ch** is pronounced like **tch** in Kreyòl; **u** like **ou** in Kreyòl.
7. A dash (-) appears before Swahili verbs which are normally preceded by the preposition **ku.**
8. **Handaki** means "tunnel" in Swahili.
9. Both Swahili and Kreyòl like to use repetition to reinforce the meaning of the word.

Futa ! Futa ! Futa jina lako.
Erase! Erase your name, damn you!
Efase! Fout! Efase non ou.

7. **Ghala**   storeroom *(depo; galta)*

Vitu viko kwenye ghala.
The things are in the storeroom.
Bagay yo nan depo/ sou galta.

8. **Hadithi**   story *(istwa)*

Hadithi ! Hadithi ! Joo!
Tim tim! Bwa chèch!

Before telling a story the Swahili narrator is wont to say: "Hadithi, hadithi." In Haïti, the narrator starts by saying "tim, tim," which could derive from the last syllable of "hadithi."

If the listeners are ready to welcome the story they reply "joo" in Swahili, meaning "come," or "bwa chèch" in Kreyòl, meaning "good firewood," a metaphor meaning "go ahead!"

9. **Hai**   not *(non; pa)*

Haitii.
Do not obey.
Pa obeyi.

Hai hai hai ! [10]
No no!
Non, non, non / Ayayay !

10. **Hapa**   here *(isit)*

Hi hapa !
Here it is !
Apa li !

---

10. Do not confuse **hai** which means "no" with **hai** which means "life." Because Swahili has many words derived from Arabic, there is **hai** meaning "life." In Hebrew, which is close to Arabic, when you wish someone good health you say: "**lahai.**" Some other examples in Swahili: **Mtu huyu yupohai**, meaning "this person is still alive." **Hayupo hai**, meaning "he is not alive." (**Haiwezekani**, meaning "it's not possible.")

11. **Jani**   leaf; grass *(fèy)*

Hataki kula kwa sababu alikula jani,[11] vyovyote…
He doesn't want to eat because he ate greens and junk food …
Li pa vle manje paske li te manje fèy, djani.…

12. **Jukwaa**   stage; platform *(platform; jouk)*

Ndege huyu yupo kwenye jukwaa.
This bird is on a platform.
Zwazo sa a sou yon jouk.

13. **Jumu**   fortune *(fòtin)*

Jumuia ni jumu.
The community is a treasure.
Kominote a se yon fòtin.

Kwa mwaka mpia, supu ya boga ni kama jumu.
In a new year pumpkin soup is like a treasure.
Nan yon nouvèl ane, soup joumou se tankou yon fòtin.

Kwa mwaka mpia kupata supu ni kupata jumu.
In a new year, finding soup is like finding a
    fortune.
Nan yon nouvèl ane, jwenn soup se jwenn fòtin.

14. **Kaba**   to squeeze; to strangle *(prije; trangle)*

Anamkaba. Anamkaba. Anamkaba !
He strangled him. He extinquished him. It is through!
Li trangle l. Li prije l. Sa kaba !

15. **Kaya**   homestead; village *(lakay, vilaj)*

Katika kaya yangu, tunaendelea vizuri.
In our village we are fine.
Nan vilaj lakay, nou anfòm.

---

11. In Swahili the letter "**j**" is pronounced the same as "**dj**" in Kreyòl.

16. **Kanzu**   robe; dressing gown for men *(rad pou gason)*

Mwanaume huyu amevaa kanzu.
That teacher wears pants.
Pwofesè sa a mete kanson.

17. **Karibu**   welcome ! *(Byenveni!)*

Caraïbes inamaanisha Karibu.
Caribbean means "welcome."
Karayib vle di Byenveni.

Karibu kwenye Caraïbes!
Welcome to the Caribbean.
Byenveni nan Karayib la!

18. **Kelele**   noise *(bri)*

Acha kelele! Acha kelele!
Shut up! Stop making noise!
Pe la! Sispann telele!

19. **Kibaka**   pickpocket *(vole; kadejakè)*

Angalia, kuna vibaka au vibwengo hapa!
Be careful, there are pickpockets or evil spirits here!
Atansyon! Gen vòlè ou baka isit la !

Kibwengo ni kama kibaka na mwizi.
An evil spirit is like a pickpocket and a thief.
Baka se tankou pikpòkèt ak vòlè.

20. **Kiboko**   something outstanding; the best; whip *(bon anpil anpil; pi bon an; fwèt)*

Mganga huyu ni kiboko kwa kuwaganga watu.
This doctor is very good at healing people.
Doktè sa a bon anpil anpil nan geri moun.

**Mganga huyu ni kiboko kwa kupata pesa;
halafu, wanamwita "boko."**

This traditional healer is good at making money; that is why they call him a "boko."
Gangan sa a bon anpil anpil nan fè kòb; se pou sa yo rele l boko.

21. **Kichocho**   feeling; a little something *(filing; yon ti bagay)*

Nipe pesa kidogo, nipe kichocho.
Give me a little change, give me a little something.
Ban m yon ti monnen, ban m yon ti tchotcho.

22. **Kichinichini**   underhandedly *(anbaanba; anbachal)*

Tunahitaji mashairi ya falsafa kuondoa ukoloni wa kichinichini.
We need philosophical poetry to uproot neo-colonialism or hidden colonialism.
Nou bezwen pwezi filozofik pou retire kolonizasyon ki la anbaanba[12] *a (neokolonialis ou kolonizasyon anba chal).*

23. **Kina**   depth *(pwofondè)*

Mizizi yao ni mrefu, wanabaki kwa kina.
The roots are long, they are upright.
Rasin yo long, yo kanpe kin.

24. **Kucha**   to respect *(respekte; respè)*

Huyu mtu ni bila kucha.
This person has no respect.
Moun sa a san respè, sankoutcha.

25. **-Lamba**   to lick *(niche)*

Mbwa analamba mkono wangu.
The dog is licking my hand.
Chyen an ap lanbe men m.

26. **Mapochopocho**   sweets *(bonbon; dous)*

Anapenda sana mapochopocho.

---

12. Both Swahili and Kreyòl repeat the same word twice in order to reinforce it.

He really likes sweets.
Li renmen bonon anpil.

Kwa hiyo wanamita "Mapocho."
That is why they call him "Mapotcho."
Se pou sa yo rele l "<u>Mapotcho</u>."[13]

27. **Mapokeo**   tradition *(tradisyon)*

Mila na mapokeo simulizi yetu ni chanzo cha akili.
Our culture and oral tradition are a source of knowledge.
Kilti ak tradisyon oral nou se yon sous konesans.

28. **Mapacha**   twins *(marasa)*

Watoto wale ni mapacha.
Those children are twins.
Ti moun sa yo se <u>marasa</u>

Kwa upande ya mila na mapokeo simulizi yetu, mapacha ambao wanakula majani hawako vizuri: wameharibika.
According to our culture and oral tradition, twins who eat leaves are not good; they get spoiled.
Daprè kilti ak tradisyon oral pa nou, <u>marasa</u> ki manje fèy pa bon: yo vin gate.

29. **Mbaya**   bad *(move)*

Kwa kawaida, kuna watu ambao hawapendi kusafisha choo. Wanafikiri kwamba ni kazi muhimu lakini ni mbaya pia. Katika Haiti, msafisha choo, anaitwa "bayakou."
In general, there are people who do not like to clean toilets. They think it's a job that is both important and bad. In Haiti, people who clean toilets are called "bayakou."
Anjeneral, gen moun ki pa renmen netwaye twalèt. Yo panse se yon travay ki alafwa enpòtan e move. An Haiti, moun ki netwaye twalèt, yo rele yo "<u>bayakou</u>."

30. **Mkojo**   urine *(pipi)*

---

13. **Mapocho** is pronounced exactly like "*mapotcho*" in Kreyòl. We have already seen Swahili and Kreyòl words with the same pronunciation.

Ni mtoto; hata sasa anakojoa kitandani.
Ni mtoto; ni nyonyo; anakojoa.
He is a child he still pees in his bed.
He is a child, an idiot, a fool.
Se yon ti moun: jiskaprezan li fè pipi nan kabann. Se yon ti moun, yon egare, yon koyo.

31. **Mola**   God *(Bon Dye)*

Mola au Mungu ni jina la Mungu.
"Mola" or "Mungu" is the name of God.
Mola ou Mungu se non Bon Dye.

Katika nchi ya Haiti, nilimjua mtu ambaye jina lake lilikuwa Mola.
In Haiti I knew a person named Mola.
Nan peyi d Haiti, m te konn yon moun yo te rele Mola.

32. **Mzimu**   dead person *(moun mouri; mò; lespri defen)*

Mtu huyu amepagawa na mzimu kwa baba yake.
That person is possessed by the spirit of his deceased father.
Moun sa a gen lwa defen papa l ki monte l.

Kwa kizulu wanaita nchi hii, Afrika ya kusini, Iningi zimu Afrika. Inamaanisha nchi ya mizimu mingi ya Afika.
In the language of Zulu they call this country South Africa or "Africa of many ancestors."
Nan lang Zoulu, yo rele peyi isit la, Afrik di Sid, ou Afrik anpil Zansèt yo. Sa vle di, se peyi anpil Zansèt Afrik yo.

33. **Nasa**   to hold; to trap *(kenbe; pyeje; pran nan nas)*

Baharini wavu wanasa.
In the ocean the net snares.
Nan lanmè filè se nas.

34. **Ndege**   bird *(zwazo)*

Wakati watu wananunua kitu shambani, kwa kawaida wanamomba mwezaji kuongeza kitu kidogo kama ndege kabla ya kumpa

hela. Kwetu, wanamomba "degi" au "bakshish" katika Tanzania.

When people are buying something in the provinces in general they ask the merchant to add something as small as a bird before paying the money. At home we call that "degi," or "bakchich" in the country of Tanzania.

Lè moun ap achte yon bagay nan pwovens, anjeneral yo mande machann nan ajoute yon kichòy ki piti tankou yon zwazo anvan yo peye kòb la. Lakay nou, yo rele sa "degi" ou "bakchich" nan peyi Tanzani.

35. **Ngumu**   difficult; fight *(difisil; goumen)*

Ni ngumu.
It's a fight.
Se yon goumen.

36. **Ondoa ukoloni**   to decolonize *(dekolonize)*

Lazima kuondoa ukoloni kwa watu wengi. Watu wale wanaitwa kasumba ya kikoloni.
Many people must be decolonized.
These people are called mental slaves.
Fòk yo dekolonize anpil moun.
Yo rele moun sa yo "esklav mantal."

Tunahitaji mashairi ya falsafa kuondoa ukoloni wa ubongo.
We need philosophical poetry for the decolonization of the mind.
Nou bezwen pwezi filozofik pou dekolonizasyon mantal.

37. **Oga**   to wash; to bathe *(benyen)*

Ataoga kwenye maji ya usheshi.
He is going to bathe in waters that have been bewitched .
Li pral benyen nan dlo wonga.

38. **Pinga**   to block; to oppose *(bloke; defann; opoze)*

Wazazi wanampinga mtoto asiende kucheza dansi.
The parents tell the child: Don't go dancing.
Paran yo di pitit la: pinga ou al danse.

39. **Piga**   beat; play music *(ritme mizik; jwe mizik)*

Wanasema: pige! Wanasema: pige!
They say: Play music! They say dance!
Yo di: Jwe mizik! Yo di: pige.[14]

40. **Piga teke**   to kick *(choute; teke)*

Anapiga teke mpira polepole.
He kicks the ball very gently.
Li teke boul la piti piti.

Mtoto anapiga teke gari kwa mguu.
The child kicked the car with his foot.
Ti moun nan teke machin nan ak pye l.

41. **Potovu / potevu**   wasteful; misguided *(potovi; petevi)*

Mtoto huyu nimpotovu sana.
That child is very misguided.
Ti moun sa a potovi anpil.

42. **Roga**   to bewitch *(fè moun mal ak wonga)*

Mchawi ameroga mtu.
That witchdoctor cast a spell to make the person sick.
Bòkò a fè moun nan malad ak wonga.

43. **Sambaa**   to be spread around *(gaye toupatou)*

Habari imesambaa kila mahali.
The news spread everywhere.
Nouvèl la gaye toupatou.

Kwetu Haïti, mtu ambaye anatunga wimbo, anaimba ili kusambaa habari kila mahali ni samba.
At home in Haïti a person who composes songs and sings to spread news everywhere is a samba.
Lakay an Ayiti, yon moun ki konpoze chante e chante pou gaye nouvèl la toupatou se yon samba.

---

14. The word **pige** is used in the South of Haiti in the same sense.

44. **Setiri**   to cover up; to keep confidential *(kouvri pou; kache; sitire)*

Huyu mtu amenisetiri wakati natafuta nyumba.
That person tolerated me and let me stay with him when I was looking for a house.
Moun sa a <u>sitire</u> m fè ladesant lè m tap chèche kay.

45. **Siga**   to contradict *(kontredi)*

Amesema: "Ninakusiga."
Anasema: "Nitakupia kusiga."
He said: "I will contradict you."
He says: "Men siga w," meaning "be my guest."[15]
Li te di: "Map kontredidi w."
Li di: "Men siga w."

46. **Tambua**   to discover *(dekouvri)*

Kwetu goma itusaidia kutambua mizizi ya Afrika.
At home, the drums help us to discover the roots of Africa.
Lakay, <u>tanbou ede n dekouvri</u> rasin Lafrik.

47. **Tete**   seed *(grenn semans)*

Titi ni kama matete.
The nipples are like seeds.
<u>Tete</u> se tankou grenn semans.

48. **Titi**   nipples *(tete)*

Titi inafanana matete.
The nipples look like seeds.
Tete sanble ak gren semans.

49. **Ulwa**   honor *(onè)*

Anasema: ni ulwa kupagawa na mzimu wa baba wake.
He said: It is an honor for his father's spirit to possess him.
Li di: se yon <u>onè pou lwa</u> papa l monte l.

---

15. The Kreyòl expression **"men siga w"** is the much cruder version of "be my guest."

50. **Wayawaya**   to totter *(mache mal; mache wayawaya)*

Anawayawaya kwa sababu amelewa pombe.
He is walking crooked because he drank alcohol.
Li mache wayawaya paske li bwè alkòl.

E) Conclusion

Behind Haïti there is Haitii

If behind mountains there are mountains,
Behind Haïti there is Haitii.

Today, mouth to mouth,
One telling the other, we must repeat
If behind mountains there are mountains,
Behind Haïti there is Haitii.

Day and night,
We must always remember
If behind mountains there are mountains,
Behind Haïti, there is Haitii.

Ulimi hauna mfupa
The tongue has no bones.

The tongue can speak and it must speak
Clearly to declare:
If behind mountains there are mountains,
Behind Haïti there is Haitii.

Ulimi unauma kuliko meno
The tongue hurts more than the teeth.

But the tongue is a medical specialist
That can heal the ears with sweet words,
Honey-sweet words, words of truth.
Our tongue will always declare:
If behind mountains there are mountains,
Behind Haïti there is Haitii.

Like our Ancestors,
Generation after generation,
We vow for all to remember
If behind mountains there are mountains,
Behind Haïti there is Haitii.

F) Appendix

Special praise for a special Mother.
The highest praises of gratitude for Mother Africa.
A love story for our Mother Africa.

Hadhiti ya mapenzi

"A love story"

Kwa hakika! Ndiyo! Bila shaka,
Wapenzi duniani watanielewa,
Kwa kuwa wao ni wapenzi.
Ni ajabu ya macho kuona jinsi
Wapenzi wanavyoweza kuelewa
Hadithi ya mapenzi duniani.

Without doubt, with no problem,
People of the world who are in love,
Will understand me because
They are people who are in love.
Isn't it beautiful when with our two eyes we can see how
Everywhere, people who know how to love
Can extract the essence from a love story.

Rafiki yangu, ingawa watu wanasema:
Pote, popote, kokote "Ndoto haidithiwi,"
Rafiki yangu, ijapokuwa wanasema:
Pote, popote, "Siri ni kwa mtu mmoja,"
Lazima kushirikiana na wewe, sasa hivi,
Ala! Hadithi yangu kuhusu Mama Afrika.

My friends, even if people often say:
"Here or far away, you don't share your dreams";
My friends, even if people often say:
"Here or not, a secret is meant for only one person,"
I must, at all costs, share with you,
A story that I experienced with Mother Africa.

Ndiyo, mimi ni mzaliwa wa mbali
Wa bahari na pwani ya Mama Afrika.
Basi! Nimekulia nchini kwetu, Haïti
Ambaye ni binti ya Mama Afrika.

Yes, I was born far, very far from
The oceans and beaches of Africa.
I grew up in my country, Haïti,
A daughter of Mother Africa.

Pale niliishi mpaka juzijuzi.
Kwa maneno mengine,
Inabidi niseme nilijitolea Haïti
Kwa maisha yangu yote.
Daima nitajitolea Haïti.

I left home only recently.
In reality, I should stress
That my whole life is for Haïti
And I will always sacrifice
My life for my country.

Kwa ghafla, ndiyo, hapa Afrika,
Kulikuwa na ziara ya kushtukiza!
Tazama hali! Angalia! Sikiliza!
Sijaona kitu chochote kama hichi.
Kamwe sijapata kuona chochote
Kilicho kizuri kama hiki. Tazama!

Suddenly, in a flash, here in Africa,
A visit that made hearts flutter, fill with joy.
Look! Open your eyes and look! Wow! Listen!
I've never seen anything like this!
I've never seen such a beautiful thing!

Wakati nilipofika hapa na familia yangu,
Mama Afrika alitupokea kwa moyo wote.
Alitubusu, alitabasamu, alicheka sana,
Alitubusu, alitugusa tena ya pili, ya tatu,
Ya nne, ya tano, daima, bila mwisho ...

As soon as I arrived here with my family,
Mother Africa cradled us in the bottom of her heart.
She embraced us, she smiled, she laughed,
She kissed us, she caressed us, touched us,
Once, twice, three times, four times, never tiring.

Pia, kufumba na kufumbua, aliniambia:
"Karibuni, watoto wangu! Habari gani?
Kumbe ! Ninyi ni watoto mnaonipendeza!

Before batting my eyes, she said
"Welcome, my children! How are you?
Wow! I am crazy about you!"

Mgeni, njoo, mwenyeji apone! Karibuni!
Come, come in! Honor for you, equals!
Respect for all that are in the house!
Mwenye moyo wa furaha, humsaidia raha!
People with a happy heart will be even happier!
Ni kweli, ndiyo, jina jema hung'ara gizani!
Yes, the name of good people can shine in the dark!
Aachaye kweli, huirudia!
He who leaves the truth shall return for it!

Kwa kweli, ukweli utabaki!
Truly, the truth will remain!

Penye nia, pana njia!
Where there is a will there is a way.

Safi sana! Safi sana!
Great! Great!

Ninyi, ni watoto wangu.
Nawapenda sana. Sana!

Mtaishi moyoni mwangu,
Inamaanisha mtakaa mbali
Kwa kasumba ya kikoloni.

You, you are my children.
I love you very much.
You will live in my heart,
That means you will stay far
Away from people who are mental slaves.

Kumbe! Mungu mwenyezi! Kumbe!
Huyu ni Mama Afrika anayenipendeza!
Kwa kifupi, mimi pia nimefurahi sana.
Moyoni, nilijisikia kama sikufika Afrika,
Lakini, nilirudi nyumbani kwa kweli.
Kwa Mama yetu, Mama Afrika, kwetu.

Wow! Oh my God!
How I love Mother Africa!
Oh, how I am happy!
From the depth of my being, I feel
That I have not *come* to Africa, but
That I have *returned* home,
Home to Mother, Mother Africa.

Inapendeza sana, sivyo? Je, ni ajabu?
Mimi pia, basi, kufumba na kufumbua,
Nilimjibu: Mpenzi Mama, Mama Afrika,
Nimeshikwa na upendo kwa ardhi yetu,
Nimeshikwa na mapenzi kwa mizizi yangu.

My friends, tell me, isn't it marvelous?
So, I too,
I answer: My dear Mother,
I cannot tell you how much I love this land,
I am passionate about my roots.

Hadithi hii, ni hadithi ya mapenzi.
Kama unavyojua, mpendwa Mama,
Kwa kweli, mapenzi ni kikohozi,
Hayawezi kufichika. Hayawezi…

Mama yetu, tuna mahaba nawe.

This story is a love story.
As you already know, my dearest Mother,
Love is like a cough,
You cannot hide it.
Mother we love you.